Blood-Bought Promises Too

Amazing Grace

Other Titles from Robert L. and Debra D. Johnson:

Blood Bought Promises of Jesus

Identity, Who Do You Think You Are?

Blood-Bought Promises Too
Amazing Grace

Robert L. and Debra D. Johnson

Kingdom Life Ministries Publishing

Dedication

This book is dedicated first to God then to my grandsons Kalib and Kadin Johnson Dua. Boys, you have inspired me to leave a written legacy of the most important things I could ever want you to know. I pray that these words will encourage and direct you to the most significant revelations one can ever receive: God loves you, and Jesus is Lord!

I also dedicate this to the BMJ family. I've often told people that when I was placed in this family, it was like winning the family lottery. Thank you, Mom and family, for your prayers, direction, and support. Finally, to my children Jamila, Jaquie, Brian, and Kapil, I love each of you more than words can express.

There were many days where I would ask myself if any of this made sense or if I should even attempt to write this. But something would be said during one of our conversations that would encourage me to keep moving forward. I thank God for you daily. And I wanted you to know that without your encouragement and unconditional love, this may not have happened. Be Blessed in Jesus' name!

Robert Johnson
AKA Pop-Pop

Dedication

I am blessed to dedicate this book to my children; Jaquie, Jamila, Brian, and Kapil; my grandboys, Kalib, and Kadin. I thank God daily for you all. I love you immensely.

Debra Johnson

Blood-Bought Promises Too Amazing Grace!

"The beginning of wisdom is: Get [skillful and godly] wisdom [it is preeminent]!

And with all your acquiring, get understanding [actively seek spiritual discernment, mature comprehension, and logical interpretation]. Proverbs 4:7 (AMP)

Getting wisdom is the wisest thing you can do! And whatever else you do, develop good judgment.

Proverbs 4:7 (NLT)

Table of Contents

Blood-Bought Promises Too

Preface

I was led to write this book because I, like many other believers, grew up in a religious environment that stressed behavior more than righteousness through faith. It all seemed normal to act like everything was perfect. But inside, I knew I could never keep all the rules. And even when I could keep them, it wasn't for very long.

The reality was, more often than not, I didn't know if God and I were in good standing at all.

I would ask myself if Jesus returned today, where would I end up: heaven or hell? This uncertainty produced condemnation and double-mindedness, which destroyed my confidence that the promises of God even applied to me. Somewhere along the way, I had misunderstood the Word of God. Somehow I had been convinced that God's love for me was dependent on me and not Christ.

With religion, the mindset of both believers and non-believers is usually one of unrighteousness; our belief becomes that God's love and approval are somehow dependent on whether we hit or miss the mark of perfection. Religion often loses sight of the fact that our justification and righteousness are through the faithfulness of Jesus. He is our substitute, and we can now come boldly to the throne of God. But unfortunately, we still often minimize the grace of God, the work of Christ, and the indwelling Holy Spirit.

Therefore, since we have been made right in God's sight by faith, we have peace with God because of what Jesus Christ our Lord has done for us. Romans 5:1 (NLT)

For he hath made him to be sin for us, who knew no sin; that we might be made the righteousness of God in him.
2 Corinthians 5:21

In this devotional, I would like to redirect your focus to the Word of God as the indisputable truth. The precious Blood of Jesus The Christ has made reconciliation with God a reality for those who believe. We now, as sons and daughters of the Most High God, have a blood-bought right to the manifested promises of God by His grace through faith in what Jesus has done on our behalf. God has given us His Word so that we will speak forth His will for His children.

The Word of God is the most powerful force in the universe! However, most of us don't possess enough rightly divided Word to impact our everyday lives.

Many have not yet discovered that the applied Word of God will shift atmospheres and adjust environments. It will rearrange your thoughts and enlarge your expectations when intimately understood: this Word of God is an absolute game-changer for those who will believe.

Therefore everyone who hears these words of mine and puts them into practice is like a wise man who built his house on the rock. Matthew 7:24 (NIV)

We must learn to rely on and believe in what God has promised.

God is not a man, that he should lie; neither the son of man, that he should repent: hath he said, and shall he not do it? or hath he spoken, and shall he not make it good? Numbers 23:19

I want everyone to catch this: the only Word that we can apply to our lives is the Word we know and understand. The Word of God is incorruptible seed that has been given to us, and, as with any other seed, it must be planted to unlock its potential. The potential for manifestation is in the planting of the seed. Only the seed that is planted is capable of producing a harvest.

God is the one who gives seed to those who plant, and he gives bread for food. And God will give you spiritual seed and make that seed grow. He will produce a great harvest from your goodness. 2 Corinthians 9:10 (ERV)

We must stop being dominated by what we see with our natural eyes and began to take God's position no matter how things appear. I took the liberty of showing this next Scripture in three versions below because everything that will be stated later in this devotional will require your faith to access God's results.

Faith is what makes real the things we hope for. It is proof of what we cannot see. Hebrews 11:1 (ERV)

Now faith is the substance of things hoped for, the evidence of things not seen. Hebrews 11:1

Now faith is the assurance (title deed, confirmation) of things hoped for (divinely guaranteed), and the evidence of things not seen [the conviction of their reality—faith comprehends as fact what cannot be experienced by the physical senses]. Hebrews 11:1 (AMP)

The Bible states in Romans 12:3 that God has given every man the measure of faith. So, we all have faith in seed form;

however, if we desire to grow that faith to the point that we live by faith, we must feed it daily.

The way to nurture our faith and plant the seed is by hearing the Word of God.

So then faith cometh by hearing, and hearing by the word of God. Romans 10:17

What we say and what we hear is crucial to the development of our faith to manifest the will of God. Inside the pages of this devotional, we have highlighted some of the most amazing promises that God ever made. And Jesus paid the price for us to take hold of them through the leading and guiding of Holy Spirit by faith.

It is our prayer that, as you read, meditate, decree, and declare these promises over your life, your family, your health, your business, your ministry, and your community, you will do so with confidence that it has never been about your perfection. But instead, it's all about what Jesus has done for us through His precious blood by the Grace of God.

Thou shalt also decree a thing, and it shall be established unto thee: and the light shall shine upon thy ways. Job 22:28

For verily I say unto you, That whosoever shall say unto this mountain, Be thou removed, and be thou cast into the sea; and shall not doubt in his heart, but shall believe that those things which he saith shall come to pass; he shall have whatsoever he saith. Mark 11:23

Therefore I tell you, whatever you ask in prayer, believe that you have received it, and it will be yours. Mark 11:24 (ESV)

This world was spoken into existence by the words of God. God said, "Light, be," and it was. This was the pattern of God; He spoke faith-filled words, and, as His children, we are to do the same. This is the blueprint God wants us to use to manifest His will in the earth. His will is that we not be tricked into believing that our words have no power. Child of God, say what God has already said about you. Be Blessed in Jesus' name!

So shall My word be that goes forth out of My mouth: it shall not return to Me void [without producing any effect, useless], but it shall accomplish that which I please and purpose, and it shall prosper in the thing for which I sent it.

Isaiah 55:11 (AMPC)

Blood-Bought Promises Too
A Daily Devotional

Introduction

In 2012 we wrote **Blood Bought Promises**, the first in a series of Holy Spirit-inspired devotionals. We began our exploration into the promises of God as a way to build faith and to encourage ourselves and others.

In **Blood Bought Promises Too**, we take a deeper look at these promises of God with a focus on Grace in the person of Jesus and our New Covenant position in Christ.

The Promises of God are the anchors of our faith. These precious promises serve not only to give us insight into the extraordinary character of God our Father, but they also allow us to behold His perfect will for His children. It is these promises that are the points of access into the faith that produces God's desired results. God's Word is God's will and, as we meditate on these sure promises of God, let us remember:

"God is not a man, that He should lie,
Nor a son of man, that He should repent.
Has He said, and will He not do it?
Or has He spoken and will He not make it good and fulfill it?" Numbers 23:19 (AMP)

But he did not doubt or waver in unbelief concerning the promise of God, but he grew strong and empowered by faith, giving glory to God, being fully convinced that God had the power to do what He had promised. Therefore his faith was credited to him as righteousness (right standing with God).

Romans 4:20-22 (AMP)

Every condition of every promise has already been met on our behalf by Jesus The Christ. We, as believers, have often misunderstood the Word of God concerning the glorious work of the Cross. We've often understated the value of what Jesus has accomplished for us.

The finished work of the Blood of Jesus has ushered in the New Covenant, whereby His work is credited to our account by God's grace and our faith in Him.

But Christ, as a Minister in heaven, has been rewarded with a far more important work than those who serve under the old laws because the new agreement that he passes on to us from God contains far more wonderful promises. Hebrews 8:6 (TLB)

Christ has perfectly positioned all who believe to access every promise of God. Because of His perfection and obedience, we can now stand in the presence of God, righteous, holy, justified, sanctified, and wise. Because of His victory, we are saved by God's grace through faith. It was never our good behavior that produced true righteousness; it was always the Blood of Jesus.

Regardless of how we tried, we could never live life without sin nature, and we could never position ourselves to access the promises of God without the work of the Blood of Jesus.

For all have sinned, and come short of the glory of God.

Romans 3:23

In fact under the Law almost everything is cleansed with blood, and without the shedding of blood there is no forgiveness [neither release from sin and its guilt, nor cancellation of the merited punishment]. Hebrews 9:22 (AMP)

He is the one who took God's wrath against our sins upon himself and brought us into fellowship with God; and he is the forgiveness for our sins and not only ours but all the world's.
1 John 2:2 (TLB)

We could never keep the perfect law that came by Moses, but Jesus could, and He did.

"Do not think that I came to do away with or undo the Law [of Moses] or the [writings of the] Prophets; I did not come to destroy but to fulfill." Matthew 5:17 (AMP)

But of him are ye in Christ Jesus, who of God is made unto us wisdom, and righteousness, and sanctification, and redemption... 1 Corinthians 1:30

For many generations, religious practices and demonic influences have attempted to eliminate dependency on Christ by faith as the only means of salvation. Religion is man's attempt to earn righteousness and the favor of God through works instead of faith. The spirits of self-righteousness and works have attacked the body of Christ using condemnation and guilt to cause believers to question their righteousness.

And so you cancel the word of God in order to hand down your own tradition. And this is only one example among many others. Mark 7:13 (NLT)

They have convinced many believers that Christ may have paid their sin debt, but that was for past sin and past iniquities. However, it is now up to us to maintain righteousness before God based on our behavior.

This lie is one of the most dangerous lies ever told to the Body of Christ.

The goal here is to destroy anything that resembles faith in the finished work of Jesus, thereby making the Word of God of no effect in the lives of many believers. We must have faith in what Christ has done to take hold of what God has already made available through His amazing grace toward us, His children.

You disregard and neglect the commandment of God, and cling [faithfully] to the tradition of men. ...so you nullify the [authority of the] word of God [acting as if it did not apply] because of your tradition which you have handed down [through the elders]. And you do many things such as that.

Mark 7:8, 13 (AMP)

The Word of God says those that Christ makes free are free indeed, John 8:36, but this freedom, this Law of liberty that's available to all, wasn't free at all. The price Jesus paid was His life, His blood, and separation from the Father. But the price we must pay as believers is a willingness to renew our minds to the true gospel of Jesus Christ, the gospel of grace brought by Apostle Paul, stated in 1 Corinthians 15:2-4.

In other words, we must be willing to allow Holy Spirit to re-train our minds to reflect God's opinion of who we are in Christ. There's a reason why God said, "Let the weak say I am strong," and to call those things that "aren't" as if they were. He's renewing our minds to His perspective, to how He sees things. He sees the end before the beginning; nothing surprises God.

And be not conformed to this world: but be ye transformed by the renewing of your mind, that ye may prove what is that good, and acceptable, and perfect, will of God. Romans 12:2

Don't change yourselves to be like the people of this world, but let God change you inside with a new way of thinking. Then you will be able to understand and accept what God wants for you. You will be able to know what is good and pleasing to him and what is perfect. Romans 12:2 (ERV)

Romans 10:17 says faith comes by hearing and hearing by the Word of God. Then hear this: Jesus paid it all! Our sins have been forgiven, past, present, and future, and God remembers them no more.

For I will be merciful to their unrighteousness, and their sins and their iniquities will I remember no more. Hebrews 8:12

God's love for us is so great that He sent His Son Jesus to shed His blood and redeem us unto Himself. He did this because He desires a perfect relationship with His children, Ephesians 1:5. The price that justice demanded was paid, and now we can come boldly to the throne of grace and place a faith demand on anything that God has promised.

Beloved, take each promise by faith. Believe what Christ has accomplished for you to the Glory of God. Trust God.

His words will never return void or fail to produce what He has spoken.

Therefore let us [with privilege] approach the throne of grace [that is, the throne of God's gracious favor] with confidence and without fear, so that we may receive mercy [for our failures] and find [His amazing] grace to help in time of need [an appropriate blessing, coming just at the right moment]. Hebrews 4:16 (AMP)

"For as the rain and snow come down from heaven, And do not return there without watering the earth, Making it bear and sprout, And providing seed to the sower and bread to the eater, So will My word be which goes out of My mouth; It will not return to Me void (useless, without result), Without accomplishing what I desire, And without succeeding in the matter for which I sent it." Isaiah 55:10-11 (AMP)

God's promises aren't there to tease us, but instead, they are there to show us God's perspective of who we already are in Christ. In Christ, God sees us as perfect, holy, acceptable, and qualified to receive His best.

The truth is we get to decide if we'll take by faith what God has made available by His grace. We are free moral agents, and we get to decide and declare how things will end based on God's Word.

"You will also decide and decree a thing, and it will be established for you; And the light [of God's favor] will shine upon your ways." Job 22:28 (AMP)

The issue with most believers has been that we have often decided to reject God's opinion of ourselves and, subsequently, we have conditioned ourselves to disagree with God. That predisposition to disagree is precisely why we must renew our minds with God's Word. If the Creator of everything says I'm forgiven, blessed, and highly favored, then I agree and declare His Word with thanksgiving. Why?

Because His Word will produce good success and never contradict His will for us. Every promise of God is "yea and amen" because of Christ's faithfulness. We're in Christ when we believe the Word of God.

For all the promises of God in him are yea, and in him Amen, unto the glory of God by us. 2 Corinthians 1:20

The Word of truth about God's grace, love, and mercy is evidence that every good thing has been made available through the Blood of Jesus. Redemption, reconciliation, sanctification, favor, and the anointing are ours in Christ.

But you have an anointing from the Holy One [you have been set apart, specially gifted and prepared by the Holy Spirit], and all of you know [the truth because He teaches us, illuminates our minds, and guards us from error]. I have not written to you because you do not know the truth, but because you do know it, and because no lie [nothing false, no deception] is of the truth. 1 John 2:20-21 (AMP)

God's Word is truth, but the manifestation is by faith, and since we know that faith comes by hearing the Word of God, we want you always to be listening. We encourage you to meditate on the promises of God, fully aware that the Blood of Jesus The Christ has qualified you to receive the inheritance God promised.

I pray that God will open your minds to see his truth. Then you will know the hope that he has chosen us to have. You will know that the blessings God has promised his holy people are rich and glorious. And you will know that God's power is very great for us who believe. It is the same as the mighty power he used to raise Christ from death and put him at his right side in the heavenly places. Ephesians 1:18-20 (ERV)

Declare by faith that you receive all that is yours by divine right through the Blood of Jesus The Christ. That is to say that everything Jesus died for us to have is our divine right, God Himself ordained it. From His perspective, salvation from hell wasn't enough. He desires that we have super-abundant lives through our relationship with Jesus led by Holy Spirit. This is the life God wants for believers, the *sozo* life; nothing missing, nothing broken.

Thayer's Greek Lexicon: sōzō: (1) to save, keep safe and sound, to rescue from danger or destruction, (1a) one (from injury or peril), (1a1) to save a suffering one (from perishing), i.e. one suffering from disease, to make well, heal, restore to health.

I am the Door; anyone who enters through Me will be saved [and will live forever], and will go in and out [freely], and find pasture (spiritual security). The thief comes only in order to steal and kill and destroy. I came that they may have and enjoy life, and have it in abundance [to the full, till it overflows].
John 10:9-10 (AMP)

Beloved, I pray that in every way you may succeed and prosper and be in good health [physically], just as [I know] your soul prospers [spiritually]. 3 John 2 (AMP)

God always has an abundance of increase in His mind; that's one of the reasons why His thoughts are higher than our thoughts. He can't conceive lack.

And God is able to make all grace [every favor and earthly blessing] come in abundance to you, so that you may always [under all circumstances, regardless of the need] have complete sufficiency in everything [being completely self-sufficient in Him], and have an abundance for every good work and act of charity. 2 Corinthians 9:8 (AMP)

For His divine power has bestowed on us [absolutely] everything necessary for [a dynamic spiritual] life and godliness, through [a] true and personal knowledge of Him who called us by His own glory and excellence. 2 Peter 1:3 (AMP)

I challenge you to grab hold of what has been made available through the incorruptible seed of God's Word. Come boldly to His throne of grace and place a faith demand on what God has made available. We overcome the enemy by the Blood of the Lamb and the Word of our testimony. The enemy could be sickness, doubt, poverty, depression, addiction, or anything else that attempts to contradict the Word of God.

We have the Blood, but we must now declare what God has said, faith declares, and we must say what we want to see. Faith is the active ingredient, and you will have what you say. What have you been saying?

We having the same spirit of faith, according as it is written, I believed, and therefore have I spoken; we also believe, and therefore speak... 2 Corinthians 4:13

The truth is, you can say to this mountain, 'Go, mountain, fall into the sea.' And if you have no doubts in your mind and believe that what you say will happen, then God will do it for you. So I tell you to ask for what you want in prayer. And if you believe that you have received those things, then they will be yours. Mark 11:23-24 (ERV)

Our prayer is that as you began to renew your mind with these blood-bought promises, you will come to know on a very personal level what is genuinely the breadth, depth, and height of God's love for you. We declare by faith that as you meditate on His Word, you will find that your true identity is in Christ, our Savior.

Believe what God already believes about you. You're more than a conqueror in Christ, Romans 8:37. You are His beloved, and He is our Father, and if an earthly father knows how to give good gifts, how much more will our heavenly Father do for His children.

Please plant the incorruptible seed of God's Word into your heart and mind by reading these promises aloud as often as possible. When we read aloud, we get the benefit of both saying the promise and hearing the promise, and that's how our faith grows. What we continually say and what we continually hear, we will eventually believe.

Then He touched their eyes, saying, "According to your faith [your trust and confidence in My power and My ability to heal] it will be done to you." Matthew 9:29 (AMP)

He touched their eyes and said, "Become what you believe." It happened. They saw. Matthew 9:29 (MSG)

So say to yourself every day, "I Am Blessed! All Is Well with Me," and "God Perfects All That Concerns Me," in Jesus' name!

Blood-Bought Promises Too

Day 1

God's Love

For God so loved the world that he gave his only begotten Son, that whosoever believeth in him should not perish, but have everlasting life. John 3:16

To begin to understand the love God has for us, we have to remove ourselves from the center of the equation. What I mean is many believers (wrongly) believe God's love for us is somehow a reward for our good works. However, the Bible says God's love is not a response to anything we did or could do. He loved us even when we rejected Him.

The truth is, God decided to love us, and, contrary to some religious teaching, God loves us unconditionally. But being the Holy God, our sin prevented the fellowship He desired, so His response to sin was the most excellent demonstration of His amazing love for us.

For if, while we were God's enemies, we were reconciled to him through the death of his Son, how much more, having been reconciled, shall we be saved through his life!

Romans 5:10 (NIV)

God has always loved us, and when I say "love," I mean it as an action word (love, the verb form). God's love for man could not be measured but is plain to see.

Jesus demonstrated God's sacrificial love on the cross as the Lamb slain to pay our sin debt. He did this so we could return to our Father and have the love relationship He intended.

Even as [in His love] He chose us [actually picked us out for Himself as His own] in Christ before the foundation of the world, that we should be holy (consecrated and set apart for Him) and blameless in His sight, even above reproach, before Him in love.

For He foreordained us (destined us, planned in love for us) to be adopted (revealed) as His own children through Jesus Christ, in accordance with the purpose of His will [because it pleased Him and was His kind intent]—

[So that we might be] to the praise and the commendation of His glorious grace (favor and mercy), which He so freely bestowed on us in the Beloved.

In Him we have redemption (deliverance and salvation) through His blood, the remission (forgiveness) of our offenses (shortcomings and trespasses), in accordance with the riches and the generosity of His gracious favor,

Which He lavished upon us in every kind of wisdom and understanding (practical insight and prudence),

Making known to us the mystery (secret) of His will (of His plan, of His purpose). [And it is this:] In accordance with His good pleasure (His merciful intention) which He had previously purposed and set forth in Him... Ephesians 1:4-9 (AMPC)

God decided before the foundation of the earth that He wanted us blameless before Him in Christ. God is so committed to loving us that 1 Peter 1:19-20 explains that God and the Word (Jesus Christ) preordained and predetermined that Jesus would become flesh and fulfill the requirements of righteousness on our behalf.

But he paid for you with the precious lifeblood of Christ, the sinless, spotless Lamb of God. God chose him for this purpose long before the world began, but only recently was he *brought into public view, in these last days, as a blessing to you.*

1 Peter 1:19-20 (TLB)

And the Word was made flesh, and dwelt among us, (and we beheld his glory, the glory as of the only begotten of the Father,) full of grace and truth. John 1:14

Jesus then went on to demonstrate (verb) His obedience to the Father and love for His creation by suffering the death and crucifixion of a guilty person even though He was sinless. Moreover, Jesus did all of this, knowing that many of the people He died for would reject His offer of forgiveness and disregard the gift.

Now, it's essential to understand that all of these details were agreed to by God the Father, Jesus the Word, and Holy Spirit. Jesus said, "the Father and I are one," so there was no friction; they were and always are in one accord.

So before any humans were ever created and being fully aware of all that they would endure, God the Father, God the Son and God the Holy Spirit made provision for us to enjoy the love they shared.

That is the purest expression of love we will ever experience. God knew it would cost Him His relationship with Jesus for a little while to have a relationship with us forever.

God has always loved us, and I say always because before there was time, God loved us, and long after time, as we know it has ceased to exist, He will love us. God said, "I will never leave you or forsake you. I am with you, always" in Hebrews 13:5.

We, as believers, must understand this truth. God loves us, and this is not some passive, dispassionate love. This love is a pure, all-encompassing love filled with promises and provision. However, the benefits of this love can only be realized and maximized through faith in God's love and the Blood of Jesus. That's how badly God wants to have an intimate, loving relationship with you. He gave His Son to clear the way for you to express His glory in Christ in you.

God's love for humankind predates man, the Ten Commandments, and the earth itself. Be Blessed!

Declaration: Father, I thank You that I am the righteousness of God in Christ Jesus. I thank You for loving me, and there is nothing that I can do to make You stop loving me, and there is nothing that I can do to make You love me more. Holy Spirit, help me to be more aware of God's love and grace toward me in Jesus' name. Amen.

Blood-Bought Promises Too

Day 2

Grace

Understanding the grace of God is of great importance to believers because the Bible states that this is how we're saved, and that the grace of God is a gift He gave freely to humanity. However, it could only be received by faith. "Faith in what?" some might ask. Well, faith in God's plan of redemption and the fact that Jesus completely executed the plan according to God's love for us. Grace is the empowerment to succeed, and it's the favor of God because He is good.

The word "grace" (*chen* in Hebrew, *charis* in Greek), as it is used in the Scriptures, literally means "favor," to bend or stoop in kindness to another as a superior to an inferior. It has the idea of graciousness in manner or action.

When used in reference to God, it is the benevolent action of Him stooping down to us in His kindness to reach us in our need, and convey upon us a benefit. His grace has been termed "Unearned kindness," but it is more than an attitude of favor or mercy. His mercy is an expression of His compassion toward us, but His grace is an extension of benevolence translated into action that releases His enabling power into our lives (wikibooks.org January 15, 2020).

Quoting from *Baker's Evangelical Dictionary of Biblical Theology,* the chapter on "Grace," "Romans 3:23-24 states quite clearly that all have fallen short of the glory of God and are 'justified freely by his grace through the redemption that came by Christ Jesus.'

"Here, while the language of the slave market may be implied in the use of the word 'redemption,' and that of the *cultus* in the use of the phrase 'sacrifice of atonement' in the next verse, the strongest linking with grace in this passage is with the word 'justified' in Romans 3:24.

"Hence the unmerited favor of God buys us legal freedom from our sin and cancels the sentence of guilt the judge has had to declare in order 'to be just and the one who justified those who have faith in Jesus' in Romans 3:26.

"It is interesting to note that the next thought of Paul is: 'where, then, is boasting? It is excluded,' Romans 3:27, again emphasizing that grace is free and not the work of man.

"In Ephesians 2:8-9, Paul states the free character of grace perhaps even more explicitly, now not using the language of justification but simply of salvation. We are told that we have been saved 'by grace' but 'through faith.' Grace is seen here as the means by which we are saved, a free gift; faith is seen as the mechanism by which that salvation or grace is appropriated. Paul must then go on to argue that even faith is 'not by works so that no one can boast,' Ephesians 2:9."

Our faith in Jesus is our assurance that the grace of God has been received in our hearts, and acknowledging the amazing grace of God is the first step to seeing the power of His favor in your life. Amen.

Declaration: Father, thank You for Your unearned favor. Thank You for justification and redemption through Jesus Christ. Thank You for the empowerment to succeed because of the leading and guiding of your Holy Spirit. I receive Your goodness by faith, and I receive freely everything Your Amazing Grace has made available in Christ by faith, in Jesus' name, Amen.

Blood-Bought Promises Too

Day 3

Forgiveness

A sin is an immoral act considered to be a transgression against divine law. However, the root of sin is a rejection of God's word and His way of doing things. When the Bible says "love one another," and instead we're evil to or hate one another, that's sin. The big issue with sin is it causes us to feel shame and guilt and disconnected in our relationships, even in our relationship with God. But now, through the death, burial, and resurrection of Jesus Christ, we can be forgiven of all our sins, past, present, and future by faith in Jesus.

That's not to say that just because God has forgiven you, there won't be natural consequences for sin behavior because there will be. If you choose to rob a bank, you'll probably go to jail. But you have God's promise that in His eyes, you are forgiven, justified, and free from spiritual guilt, because Jesus paid your sin debt.

So let it be clearly known by you, brothers, that through Him forgiveness of sins is being proclaimed to you; and through Him everyone who believes [who acknowledges Jesus as Lord and Savior and follows Him] is justified and declared free of guilt from all things, from which you could not be justified and freed of guilt through the Law of Moses. Acts 13:38-39 (AMP)

Religion has often misunderstood forgiveness. The Merriam-Webster dictionary defines *forgive* as "to cease to harbor resentment toward an offender or to grant relief from payment."

However, in the Bible, Jesus takes this concept of forgiveness even further than just ceasing to harbor resentment against an offender. In the Bible, it doesn't state that Jesus relieves us of our obligation, as in forbearance, or that somehow God just forgave us due to some form of pity. The Bible says that Jesus made the payment for our sins on our behalf. There is quite a distinction between these two processes, because when someone pays what is rightfully owed by you, then you no longer owe the debt. For instance, if I pay for your meal, the restaurant is no longer seeking payment from you.

That is what Jesus did for the entire world. He paid the sin debt for all humanity, but unfortunately, not everyone will accept the payment.

For He has rescued us and has drawn us to Himself from the dominion of darkness, and has transferred us to the kingdom of His beloved Son, in whom we have redemption [because of His sacrifice, resulting in] the forgiveness of our sins [and the cancellation of sins' penalty]. Colossians 1:13-14 (AMP)

We praise Jesus for what He has made available through the work on the cross. We, as believers, can now operate from a position of a right relationship with God our Father. Because of the Blood of Jesus, sin is no longer a barrier to all that God desires for us. Be Blessed!

Therefore, there is now no condemnation for those who are in Christ Jesus... Romans 8:1 (NIV)

Declaration: Father, I thank You for Your grace and mercy. I thank You for Jesus and the sacrifice made on my behalf. Because of Your love, I am forgiven, and I receive by faith everything that You have made available to me in Christ, in the name of Jesus. Amen.

Blood-Bought Promises Too

Day 4

Righteousness

The Merriam-Webster Dictionary defines *righteous* as "acting in accord with divine or moral law: free from guilt or sin."

We, as believers, often think of righteousness as something that we must somehow conjure. We've been led to believe righteousness is our responsibility and that if we don't make ourselves righteous through our actions, we have no part with God. But that couldn't be further from the truth.

We've been taught that our right standing or worthiness before God was determined by our behavior. But the truth is, there is no amount of good behavior or no amount of kind acts that can ever make us righteous before God, our creator. The truth is, when we attempt to bear the standard of righteousness apart from Christ, we fall into what's known as self-righteousness.

Knowing that a man is not justified by the works of the law, but by the faith of Jesus Christ, even we have believed in Jesus Christ, that we might be justified by the faith of Christ, and not by the works of the law: for by the works of the law shall no flesh be justified. Galatians 2:16

Self-righteousness is a great offense to God because it, in effect, negates what Jesus has done and signals, "I don't accept the payment made on my behalf,"; basically, "I got this, God."

But the Word is specific. Jesus has been made righteousness for us! His righteousness is credited to our account by faith in Him. Our good behavior or bad behavior won't qualify or disqualify us from righteousness. It's always been the work of Jesus on the cross that makes us righteous.

Now, that's not to say that how we behave doesn't matter. There are always natural consequences for our actions, but just as we were born sinners by the actions of one man, Adam, we are made righteous by the actions of one man Jesus Christ.

This righteousness of God comes through faith in Jesus Christ for all those [Jew or Gentile] who believe [and trust in Him and acknowledge Him as God's Son]. There is no distinction... Romans 3:22 (AMP)

But of him are ye in Christ Jesus, who of God is made unto us wisdom, and righteousness, and sanctification, and redemption... 1 Corinthians 1:30

I want to belong to him. In Christ I am right with God, but my being right does not come from following the law. It comes from God through faith. God uses my faith in Christ to make me right with him. Philippians 3:9 (ERV)

But to him that worketh not, but believeth on him that justifieth the ungodly, his faith is counted for righteousness.
Romans 4:5

Be Blessed!

Declaration: Father God, I thank You for righteousness through the Blood of Jesus. Because of Your love for me, I come boldly to Your throne of grace, free of guilt and condemnation. Holy Spirit, I invite You to teach, lead, and guide me to the plan You have for my life. I am the righteousness of God in Christ Jesus, and All is well with me in Jesus' name. Amen.

Blood-Bought Promises Too

Day 5

Holy Spirit/God in Us

Many believers miss the main point of the death, burial, and resurrection of Jesus. We know that Christ died for our sins, but that's not the whole story. Our sin was preventing God from having the relationship that He desired with His family, which was for us to be one with Him. This desire was also what Jesus prayed in John 17.

"My prayer is not for them alone. I pray also for those who will believe in me through their message, that all of them may be one, Father, just as you are in me and I am in you. May they also be in us so that the world may believe that you have sent me? I have given them the glory that you gave me, that they may be one as we are one." John 17:20-22 (NIV)

God wanted His spirit to dwell in us, to live inside us in the person of His Holy Spirit. But this would only be possible if our sin debt was paid, and since we could never pay it ourselves. God sent His Son in the flesh to pay in blood for all humanity. All of this happened because God wants His spirit and our spirits to be one. Holy Spirit is the evidence of God's love for us, and the Blood of Jesus was the means for God's will to be done.

And if the Spirit of Him Who raised up Jesus from the dead dwells in you, [then] He Who raised up Christ Jesus from the dead will also restore to life your mortal (short-lived, perishable) bodies through His Spirit Who dwells in you.

Romans 8:11 (AMPC)

For God wanted them to know that the riches and glory of Christ are for you Gentiles, too. And this is the secret: Christ lives in you. This gives you assurance of sharing his glory.

Colossians 1:27 (NLT)

Holy Spirit, in us, is the evidence of God's love and amazing grace towards us.

And he was withdrawn from them about a stone's cast, and kneeled down, and prayed, Saying, Father, if thou be willing, remove this cup from me: nevertheless not my will, but thine, be done. Luke 22:41-42

Jesus' Blood was shed so that we could receive the indwelling of God's spirit. Please don't neglect the relationship and daily fellowship with God's Holy Spirit. He wants to lead and guide us to the truth of who we really are in Christ.

But the Comforter (Counselor, Helper, Intercessor, Advocate, Strengthener, Standby), the Holy Spirit, Whom the Father will send in My name [in My place, to represent Me and act on My behalf], He will teach you all things. And He will cause you to recall (will remind you of, bring to your remembrance) everything I have told you. John 14:26 (AMPC)

But when He, the Spirit of Truth comes, He will guide you into all the truth [full and complete truth]. For He will not speak on His own initiative, but He will speak whatever He hears [from the Father—the message regarding the Son], and He will disclose to you what is to come [in the future].

John 16:13 (AMP)

Be Blessed!

Declaration: Holy Spirit, thank You for Your presence, and thank You for leading and guiding me into all truth. I ask that You direct every area of my life. I declare that because You teach me, I live the abundant life You've planned for me, in Jesus' name. Amen.

Blood-Bought Promises Too

Day 6

Peace

God has promised the believer peace that surpasses understanding, but it doesn't just happen. We must keep our minds focused on Jesus.

Thou wilt keep him in perfect peace, whose mind is stayed on thee: because he trusteth in thee. Isaiah 26:3

Most of us think that peace is a byproduct of a life free from ups and downs, but the truth is that peace doesn't come by way of a trouble-free life. Peace actually comes from what you know. That's why Isaiah said, "He will keep thee in perfect peace" when you have your mind on Jesus, also known as the Word, John 1:1.

You need to know that the truth that will keep you in perfect peace is in the Word of God.

In every situation we face, we have the ability to choose where we focus our attention. When we choose to focus on the Word, it becomes the anchor of our peace. However, for many believers choosing to worry (which is negative meditation) is more familiar. God has spoken promised provision for everything that comes to attack our peace, But we have to decide and then decree according to the word of God. We have to say what God says; we have to agree in faith. Remember, if it cost you your peace, it's too expensive.

"No weapon that is formed against you will succeed; And every tongue that rises against you in judgment you will condemn. This [peace, righteousness, security, and triumph over opposition] is the heritage of the servants of the Lord, And this is their vindication from Me," says the Lord. Isaiah 54:17 (AMP)

The peace that Christ gives is to guide you in the decisions you make; for it is to this peace that God has called you together in the one body. And be thankful. Colossians 3:15 (GNT)

Happiness is often dependent on happenings or events, but peace is a byproduct of knowing and believing the Word of God. Apply the Word of God to every thought or circumstance that seeks to invade your thinking and disrupt your peace. Jesus said, "Peace I give to thee." Receive it by faith. Be Blessed!

Declaration: Holy Spirit, I thank You for helping me keep my mind on the Word of Your promise today, regardless of what it looks like. I declare I operate in Your peace daily. I bind every attack against my peace by word or deed. All is well with me in Jesus' name! Amen.

Bought-Promises Too

Day 7

New Creation

I know that it's a mystery, but when we accept Jesus as our personal Savior, we become a new creation. Now, everyone that believes has heard this Scripture, but I'm not sure we truly understand what it means.

Therefore if any person is [ingrafted] in Christ (the Messiah) he is a new creation (a new creature altogether); the old [previous moral and spiritual condition] has passed away. Behold, the fresh and new has come!

2 Corinthians 5:17 (AMPC)

In Genesis 1:26, we see our status as a new creation is truly in the spiritual image of God. We are new because we have a regenerated spirit, a spirit that looks just like God the Father, God the Son, and God, the Holy Spirit.

Our human spirit is now governed by the indwelling Spirit of God, which means we now have the capacity to have the same mind as Jesus.

Let this mind be in you, which was also in Christ Jesus..."

Philippians 2:5

However, this process only takes place as we began to renew our minds to the truth of Jesus.

Don't copy the behavior and customs of this world, but let God transform you into a new person by changing the way you think. Then you will learn to know God's will for you, which is good and pleasing and perfect. Romans 12:2 (NLT)

Before God awakened our spirit, man could never share the mind of God. But, here we are told to have the same mind as Jesus. Moreover, we also share the new creature status in that we can now operate in the same power that raised Christ from the dead.

And [I pray] that the eyes of your heart [the very center and core of your being] may be enlightened [flooded with light by the Holy Spirit], so that you will know and cherish the hope [the divine guarantee, the confident expectation] to which He has called you, the riches of His glorious inheritance in the saints (God's people), and [so that you will begin to know] what the immeasurable and unlimited and surpassing greatness of His [active, spiritual] power is in us who believe. These are in accordance with the working of His mighty strength which He produced in Christ when He raised Him from the dead and seated Him at His own right hand in the heavenly places.
Ephesians 1:18-20 (AMP)

"We now also have a blood-bought right to be sons and daughters of God and claim our rightful position as royalty and citizens of the Kingdom of God. Being a new creature has very little to do with physical appearances and everything to do with faith in the Word of God
And I will be a Father to you,
And you will be My sons and daughters,"
Says the Lord Almighty. 2 Corinthians 6:18 (AMP)

Last but not least, this new creature status brings with it: Righteousness, Redemption, Sanctification, Wisdom, and God will no longer remember your sins or iniquities. The New Creature status provides all the Blessings of God and no curses.

But of him are ye in Christ Jesus, who of God is made unto us wisdom, and righteousness, and sanctification, and redemption... 1 Corinthians 1:30

Now! Expect more than ever before; after all, you are a New Creature, and your identity is in Christ. Whatever He is, you are; whatever He has, you have. You are as He is in this world, meaning you will operate in dominion and authority when you better understand your new identity and position in Christ. We are co-heirs and co-laborers, seated with Him spiritually in Heaven. Be Blessed!

"Our standing in the world is identical with Christ's."
From 1 John 4:17-18 (MSG)

Declaration: Thank You, Father, for my new identity in Christ Jesus. Holy Spirit, help me to renew my mind to the truth of who I am now in Christ, and what the Blood of Jesus has accomplished on my behalf. I receive freely all that is mine as a son/daughter of the Most High God in Jesus' name! Amen.

Blood-Bought Promises Too

Day 8

The Power to Choose

Every time I think about God, I love and appreciate Him more. When He gave us dominion over the earth, He also gave us the means and ways to exercise this right to decide. You see, that's part of what dominion is: the right to choose.

You will also decide and decree a thing, and it will be established for you; And the light [of God's favor] will shine upon your ways. Job 22:28 (AMP)

And God said, Let us make man in our image, after our likeness: and let them have dominion over the fish of the sea, and over the fowl of the air, and over the cattle, and over all the earth, and over every creeping thing that creepeth upon the earth. Genesis 1:26

We as free moral agents get to decide if we are going to act in our role as Deciders, or if we are going to stand back and be Spectators in our own lives, waiting on God to decide something for us that He already decided a long time ago.

And God blessed them and said to them, Be fruitful, multiply, and fill the earth, and subdue it [using all its vast resources in the service of God and man]... Genesis 1:28 (AMPC)

God is now waiting for believers to decide to agree with Him. Joshua tells us to "choose you this day whom you will serve," in Joshua 24:15. In other words, decide who you're going to agree with, God or lost man. (Ye shall decide and decree it, and it will be established, Job 22:28.)

The ball is really in the court of the believer. We can, on purpose, choose to accept everything that the Blood of Jesus has made available. We can also decide on purpose to agree with God that every promise made in His Word is yes and amen to those who believe.

And if it seem evil unto you to serve the Lord, choose you this day whom ye will serve. Joshua 24:15

God is not a man, and He cannot lie. When He gave us dominion, it's because He wants us to use it. As a matter of fact, that's one of the things that Jesus took back on the cross. Christ stripped Satan of the authority that he had stolen from Adam. Now, through Christ, believers can operate in their God-given authority as Deciders.

I know that this may come as a surprise to many, but God is not doing anything else in general. We see that God sat down after completing creation, and in John 19, Jesus declares, "it is finished," and then He took His seat at the right hand of the Father. So, everything that the Triune God: Father, Son, and Holy Spirit, promised is already in place; however, now it's up to us to decide to allow Holy Spirit to lead and direct us to everything God had predestined before the world ever existed.

Adam was created to be a Decider. He named everything, and the Bible says that what He called a thing is what it was. What are you deciding? What are you calling things? You can open your mouth and agree with God that you are blessed, anointed, forgiven, prosperous, and healed. Decide it and decree it today! Be Blessed!

Declaration: Father God, thank You for blessing me with the authority to decide and the precious name of Jesus. I receive by faith Your Holy Spirit wisdom to make decisions that move me into the destiny that You have called me to in Jesus' name! Amen.

Blood-Bought Promises Too

Day 9

The Name of Jesus

God gave Jesus a name that is above every name in heaven and Earth (Philippians 2:9). This name causes devils and demons to tremble when spoken. God Almighty has given us this name to ensure that what we ask in Jesus' name is granted to us.

And I will do whatever you ask in my name, so that the Father may be glorified in the Son. You may ask me for anything in my name, and I will do it. John 14:13-14 (NIV)

There's only one condition, and it's this: we must believe we receive when we ask, not when we see it. But for many of us, it's hard to believe we've received before we actually possess something. Also, too often, our perception of ourselves is that some of our actions have disqualified us from our blood-bought right to ask, and use the name of Jesus.

For this reason I am telling you, whatever things you ask for in prayer [in accordance with God's will], believe [with confident trust] that you have received them, and they will be given to you. Mark 11:24 (AMP)

Well, that couldn't be further from the truth. Your self-righteousness could never qualify you to use the name of Jesus, and the fact that you're not perfect doesn't disqualify you. The Blood of Jesus qualifies you to use the name of Jesus and further qualifies you to have every prayer prayed in the name of Jesus answered in the affirmative.

For it is from God alone that you have your life through Christ Jesus. He showed us God's plan of salvation; he was the one who made us acceptable to God; he made us pure and holy and gave himself to purchase our salvation.

1 Corinthians 1:30 (TLB)

God will withhold no good thing from us, and His Word is His will. Pray the Word of God; say what He's said about you. The name of Jesus is our authority to command on this Earth. When we combine His sovereignty and our faith-filled words, everything must line up with the Word of God and the name of Jesus. God gave us the name of Jesus, and when you use the King's name, you get the King's treatment. Praise Jesus! Be Blessed!

That at the name of Jesus every knee should bow, of things in heaven, and things in earth, and things under the earth And that every tongue should confess that Jesus Christ is Lord, to the glory of God the Father. Philippians 2:10-11

Declaration: Father, I thank You for the name of Jesus. I believe that every good thing I pray in His name must be provided to me. I thank You for the manifestations of the Blessing in every area of my life. Holy Spirit, I ask that You teach me to pray God's will for my life and guide me in my purpose, in Jesus' name! Amen.

Blood-Bought Promises Too

Day10

Strength

We as people tend to grow weary from the daily battles that take place in our lives. We often hear the phrase, "if it's not one thing, it's another." Although we may feel like we lack the energy to carry the burden of even one more issue, it's important to remember that all the promises of God are "yea and amen" for those who believe.

Do not grieve, for the joy of the Lord is your strength.
Nehemiah 8:10 (NIV)

God has given every believer a secret weapon: it's the joy of the Lord. Whenever believers reflect on all that the Blood of Jesus has provided for us, it gives us the strength and confidence to press forward. When we take time to thank God for all that is right in our lives, it emphasizes what Jesus has given us access to through His blood.

Be encouraged that no matter how weary you may be at this moment, please remember this, too, will pass. We can take rest, knowing that God perfects all that concerns us, as He declares in Psalm 138:8.

The strength we need to be victorious in life is in a personal relationship with Christ.

I can do all things [which He has called me to do] through Him who strengthens and empowers me [to fulfill His purpose—

I am self-sufficient in Christ's sufficiency; I am ready for anything and equal to anything through Him who infuses me with inner strength and confident peace.]

Philippians 4:13 (AMP)

The Bible tells us in 1 Peter 5:7 to roll our cares onto Christ because "He cares for you." I used to think that this meant that Jesus cares for me as in "He loves me." Which is true, but that is not what that Scripture means to me. I believe that because of God's law of substitution, when I can let go and trust God as faithful to His Word, Jesus will care in my place. And let's face it; He is far more suited to address your cares than you are.

Do not fear [anything], for I am with you;
Do not be afraid, for I am your God.
I will strengthen you, be assured I will help you;
I will certainly take hold of you with My righteous right hand [a hand of justice, of power, of victory, of salvation].

Isaiah 41:10(AMP)

When we ask God how to manage our cares, Holy Spirit will begin to lead and direct us to the solutions to issues that rob us of our focus and strength. Focus on what Christ has done, and your joy will be full, and that joy will be your strength. Be Blessed!

But the Lord is faithful, and He will strengthen you [setting you on a firm foundation] and will protect and guard you from the evil one. 2 Thessalonians 3:3 (AMP)

Declaration: Father God, thank You for giving me energy and strength in my physical body to master every challenge today. Holy Spirit, help me to decide to take no care for the issues of today. I declare that All Is Well with me, and God is perfecting all that concerns me, in Jesus' name! Amen.

Blood-Bought Promises Too

Day 11

Wisdom

We are living in a time where the need to make choices comes at us faster than ever and in real-time. With so much conflicting information, how can we, as believers, know that we're making sound decisions?

When we have important matters to decide, and we don't know which direction to turn, we don't have to make those decisions in the dark. You see, God has provided wisdom through the Blood of Jesus. The Bible tells us that Christ has become wisdom for those who believe.

*But it is from Him that you are in Christ Jesus, who became to us wisdom from God...*1 Corinthians 1:30 (AMP)

Now, I have a personal definition of wisdom. I call it a "Rob-ism," which is a definition Holy Spirit has shared with me to help me to simplify a concept. The Rob-ism for Wisdom is knowing what to do, how to do, when to do, and with whom. This insight, which is already known by Holy Spirit, is available to anyone who asks for it. The Bible says if anyone lacks wisdom, let him ask God, and He will give it liberally.

If any of you lacks wisdom [to guide him through a decision or circumstance], he is to ask of [our benevolent] God, who gives to everyone generously and without rebuke or blame, and it will be given to him. James 1:5 (AMP)

Here God has promised to provide us with insight and direction to know how to respond to every situation we face in life. Now, this doesn't mean that you won't ever make a wrong choice or fail to use wisdom in the future, but what it will do is make us more sensitive to the things God wants us to do, which will always be the wisest choice.

When we ask God for wisdom, we are agreeing with God that He has the wisdom to give and is, in fact, the only source of wisdom. The Bible states in Proverbs 3:6 that in all our ways, if we acknowledge God as wisdom, He will direct our paths.

This is a safeguard that God has made available to believers so we can avoid the pits and snares that trip us up or trap us in the results of bad choices.

For His divine power has bestowed on us [absolutely] everything necessary for [a dynamic spiritual] life and godliness, through true and personal knowledge of Him who called us by His own glory and excellence. 2 Peter 1:3 (AMP)

God gives wisdom and everything else we need to thrive in life; it's yours for the asking.

Ask, and it shall be given you; seek, and ye shall find; knock, and it shall be opened unto you: For every one that asketh receiveth; and he that seeketh findeth; and to him that knocketh it shall be opened. Matthew 7:7-8

Be Blessed!

Declaration: Father, thank You for Your faithfulness toward me and your promises. I ask You for Your wisdom to know what to do regardless of the situation. Thank You, Holy Spirit, for Your guidance and direction. I believe I receive spiritual downloads that give me an advantage in every situation. I believe I have favor with You and man today, in Jesus' name, Amen.

Blood-Bought Promises Too

Day 12

Desires

There is a Scripture, Psalm 37:4, that says that God gives us the desires of our hearts.

For many years I misunderstood this Scripture. I believed that it meant that if I wanted something, God would give it to me. Now, that's not necessarily a wrong perspective, but it's not accurate as it pertains to this Scripture. You see, many believers live disgruntled and frustrated lives filled with disappointment because they have misguided expectations.

Hope deferred makes the heart sick, But when desire is fulfilled, it is a tree of life. Proverbs 13:12 (AMP)

We spend our lives with a wish list of things as though God was some kind of genie in a bottle. Well, that couldn't be further from the truth. What I've come to understand is that dreams to do great things, those ideas that you have to help and bless people, or that longing in your heart to start that nursery, or to write that book, or to start that ministry—those desires came from God.

The Lord directs the steps of the godly. He delights in every detail of their lives. Psalm 37:23 (NLT)

That's what the Scripture is trying to get across to us, not that anything we want God will give us. But that those good things, those too-big-to-come-true dreams, those ideas to create, serve, and provide for others, those are God's desires, and He placed them in your heart as seeds, and He will direct us as we nurture and develop them and they will produce the image of God.

God gives us the desires of our hearts in line with His purpose. By the way, God is always trying to move us to our best lives now, and the desires that keep tugging at your heart might be a hint from God.

Psalm 35:27 states that God takes pleasure in our prosperity, and the way we move into areas of prosperity is to pay close attention to the desires God has put in our hearts, or spirit man. "In all thy ways acknowledge Him, and He will direct our path," Proverb 3:6, to the desires He's deposited in our hearts.

These desires manifested will reveal your purpose, your assignment, and your anointing. I don't know what desires are in your heart, but ask Holy Spirit to direct and guide you into everything God is calling you to.

Now unto him that is able to do exceeding abundantly above all that we ask or think, according to the power that worketh in us. Ephesians 3:20

Be Blessed!

Declaration: Father, thank You for giving me good desires, and thank You for ordering my steps according to my purpose. I declare in the name of Jesus that all is well with me because of the blood. I will realize all that You've deposited in me because of Your Holy Spirit in Jesus' name! Amen.

48

Blood-Bought Promises Too

Day 13

Sound Mind

God says in Scripture that He has given us a sound mind, 2 Timothy 1:7, but what does that really mean? Well, for me, a sound mind was coming to an understanding that there was often more than one conversation taking place in my thoughts. I couldn't explain it, but I knew it was spiritual because they were frequently conflicting ideas.

Then, one day, I got a revelation in the simplest way.

Someone told me that any thought that doesn't line up with the Word of God was not of God. Strangely enough, the lightbulb came on, and from that day forward, I began to measure every thought in the context of the Word.

The Bible says to "cast down any thought that opposes knowledge of God" and to "take every thought captive to the obedience of God," 2 Corinthians 10:5.

Now, I better understand that this is one of the keys to a sound mind, but the key only works when we know what God has said. Only the truth destroys deception.

By taking every thought, decision, and belief through the filter of the Word of God, we maintain the soundness of our minds. The attacks against our minds are the negative thoughts that produce fear, guilt, shame, and hopelessness. When this happens, we must not allow that thought to take root. We must immediately replace it with what God has said. If thoughts of lack bombard your mind, declare that God supplies everything you need. If fear comes, say aloud, "God did not give me the spirit of fear." The spoken Word of God will stop attacks in your thoughts.

Casting down imaginations, and every high thing that exalteth itself against the knowledge of God, and bringing into captivity every thought to the obedience of Christ...

2 Corinthians 10:5

You see, a sound mind is when you can distinguish God's voice from all the other voices. We are the most sound of mind when we think like God. But the problem is that we've thought in opposition to God for so long it has become our natural default.

However, God says that we can renew our minds with His Word; we can have the mind of Christ. This transformation is possible because of the Blood of Jesus. Because of Jesus, we have a blood-bought right to a sound mind.

Don't copy the behavior and customs of this world, but be a new and different person with a fresh newness in all you do and think. Then you will learn from your own experience how his ways will really satisfy you. Romans 12:2 (TLB)

God is not the author of confusion, and He didn't design us to be confused in our Soul (mind, will, or emotions). Christ came that we should be made free. He did all the work. Our job is to believe.

Now renew your mind, God's will is that you prosper and be in good health even as your soul prospers. Our minds are most at peace when we can hear God and allow Holy Spirit to lead and guide.

My sheep hear my voice, and I know them, and they follow me. John 10:27

Beloved, I wish above all things that thou mayest prosper and be in health, even as thy soul prospereth. 3 John 2

To live life with God on mute leaves us in darkness and subject to the wrong voices. You have a blood-bought right to a mind not always under attack, a mind free to hear from and serve God, Amen. And Be Blessed!

Declaration: Father, I thank You for a sound mind, I have the mind of Christ. Thank You that no thought or idea will change my mind about who You are or who I am in Christ through the blood. I decree that all is well with me, and no weapon formed shall prosper against me. Thank You, Holy Spirit, for directing me in my thoughts and decisions in Jesus' name! Amen.

Blood-Bought Promises Too

Day 14

God Hears Your Prayers

One of the worst things that can happen to a believer is to find yourself in a situation where the only answer is divine intervention, but you lack the faith to believe. It's tough when you cry out to God only to wonder if He heard you; moreover, if He heard you, will He answer your prayers?

Contrary to what many of us have believed, there are not three ways that God answers prayers. I've heard it taught that God's answers are either yes, no, or not now. But the Bible states that every promise to the believer is "yea and amen," 2 Corinthians 1:20. So, what type of prayer is God not answering?

The Bible says that God's words will not return void, Isaiah 55:11, so any prayer that gives God's word back to Him, He promises to say yes to; which, by default, means any request that is not His word He has no obligation to hear or answer. The Bible tells us that angels respond to the word of God, so if there's no word of God, there will be no response.

Bless the Lord, you His angels,
Who excel in strength, who do His word,
Heeding the voice of His word. Psalm 103:20 (NKJV)

It is important to note that God does not respond to our pleading or begging. God responds to the Word, so answered prayer is not a byproduct of your sincerity or desperation; it's a result of your belief in God's faith-filled words. Our prayer life has to be rooted in the Word, or Promises of God.

You see, every word that God spoke is a promise. It's a solemn oath or guarantee to perform because God cannot lie. So, when we read that, "if God hears you, He will answer you," and "if He answers you based on something He said," then the answer can only be "yes."

For as many as are the promises of God, in Christ they are [all answered] "Yes." So through Him we say our "Amen" to the glory of God. 2 Corinthians 1:20 (AMP)

God promised that His Word would never return void but would always produce, and our prayer life is an excellent opportunity to practice being like our Father. Say what God says and get God's guaranteed results.

As believers, we cannot just come to God with a list of needs and issues. We have to study the Word, so we are equipped to respond to any condition, situation, or issue with prayer rooted in the blood-bought promises.

In the book of Hebrews and Philippians, we are instructed to come boldly to the throne and make our request known. However, this boldness should come from an absolute understanding that the Blood of Jesus has positioned you to put a faith demand on the promises of God.

In Christ, God hears you, and the answer to every promise is "yes."

Now, I need you to know that your actions, acts of self-righteousness, or religious rituals have no place in qualifying you to have your prayers heard. It is Jesus alone who positions us. Our job is to know what God has said and remind Him of His Word, not because He forgot, but because man, as the authority in the earth, we release God's Word to give God permission to govern our lives.

Similar to when Mary was approached by the Spirit and told that she would be the mother of Jesus, she gave God permission when she said, "Be it done to me as you have spoken in Luke 2." When we say to God what He has said to us, we agree and permit Him to move in our lives.

God will never move contrary to His Word. His Word is His Will, and when you pray His Word, you're saying, "Be it done unto me as you have spoken"; and that prayer He promises to answer. Pray the Word and declare that God perfects everything that concerns you. And Be Blessed!

Declaration: Holy Spirit, thank You for helping me to remember Your Word when I pray. I thank You for faith-filled words that put Jesus at the center of my prayers. I decree I pray perfect prayers in line with my purpose and the will of God in Jesus' name! Amen.

PS: Holy Spirit brought to my attention that I hadn't mentioned praying in Tongues. Well, this gift of the prayer language is available to every born-again believer. If you haven't received the gift of tongues, I encourage you to ask Holy Spirit to lead you into this powerful gift. Holy Spirit will give you perfect prayers that are always in line with God's will for your life, even when you don't know what to pray.

And the Holy Spirit helps us in our weakness. For example, we don't know what God wants us to pray for. But the Holy Spirit prays for us with groanings that cannot be expressed in words. And the Father who knows all hearts knows what the Spirit is saying, for the Spirit pleads for us believers in harmony with God's own will. Romans 8:26-27 (NLT)

Blood-Bought Promises Too

Day 15

The Blessing

In Genesis 1, God declares the Blessing upon humankind, and this Blessing was given to empower humanity to fulfill God's mission on the earth and do so without sweat and toil. The Blessing bestowed authority and dominion upon man by God's design, so we who believe are blessed.

And God blessed them [granting them certain authority] and said to them, "Be fruitful, multiply, and fill the earth, and subjugate it [putting it under your power]; and rule over (dominate) the fish of the sea, the birds of the air, and every living thing that moves upon the earth." Genesis 1:28 (AMP)

When God told Adam to subdue the earth, He gave him the ability to complete the mission. But as we all know, Adam decided to disobey God, and the relationship that created this ability to succeed was interrupted. From that point forward, man had to work very hard to have what God had given them freely.

God never asked Adam to earn the Blessing; he freely received what God made available. That was fully displayed in his decision to disobey because, in making that choice, he acknowledged his free moral agency, his God-given right to choose. Unfortunately, he chose wrong.

But God, with His love and faithfulness, never changed His mind about His desire to bless us. So, in His infinite wisdom,

He put in place a system of divine substitution so He could legally continue to bless His creation.

For God does not change his mind about whom he chooses and blesses. Romans 11:29 (GNT)

But, this system was not God's best; it was just a type or shadow or preview of what was to come. God had a solution to repairing the relationship, so the fullness of the Blessing would operate in our lives again.

This restoration came by way of the Blood of Jesus. God loves us so much that He sent Jesus to repair the breach so that everything that the Blessing was supposed to produce is available to believers today.

And in accordance with this will [of God] we [who believe in the message of salvation] have been sanctified [that is, set apart as holy for God and His purposes] through the offering of the body of Jesus Christ (the Messiah, the Anointed) once for all.
Hebrews 10:10 (AMP)

Jesus re-instituted the Blessing, and this empowerment to succeed is designed to direct us to where we are to be. It connects us to the people and provisions we need to fulfill our purpose and protects us from attacks against us operating in our purpose.

And God is able to make all grace [every favor and earthly blessing] come in abundance to you, so that you may always [under all circumstances, regardless of the need] have complete sufficiency in everything [being completely self-sufficient in Him], and have an abundance for every good work and act of charity. Corinthians 9:8 (AMP)

For by one offering he hath perfected for ever them that are sanctified. Hebrews 10:14

You see, if you can believe that Jesus successfully reinstated the Blessing, then you have full access to this empowerment to succeed. Real success starts with understanding your position in Christ. There is no curse for those in Christ.

Christ purchased our freedom and redeemed us from the curse of the Law and its condemnation by becoming a curse for us—for it is written, "Cursed is everyone who hangs [crucified] on a tree (cross)..." Galatians 3:13 (AMP)

If you have accepted Jesus as your Savior, you should be expecting good all the time, and everywhere you go.

For I know the thoughts that I think toward you, saith the Lord, thoughts of peace, and not of evil, to give you an expected end. Jeremiah 29:11

And all these blessings shall come on thee, and overtake thee, if thou shalt hearken unto the voice of the Lord thy God.
Deuteronomy 28:2

Agree with God that you are Blessed!

Declaration: Thank You, Father, for providing the Blessing by and through Jesus. Holy Spirit, help me to acknowledge and operate in the Blessing. I declare I live in the Blessing of the Lord every day; God favors me in Jesus' name! Amen.

Blood-Bought Promises Too

Day 16

Seed, Time and Harvest

Giving has often been a sore subject in some churches, and amongst some believers, much of the issue is that many of us don't understand God's economy. God has put in place spiritual, natural, and scientific laws and principles that govern the spiritual realm, Earth, and humanity.

While the earth remaineth, seedtime and harvest, and cold and heat, and summer and winter, and day and night shall not cease. Genesis 8:22

One of these principles has to do with how God has chosen to meet the needs of man. It's worth noting that God's idea of increase is the same regardless of what's being increased. God's method is the same whether you want more corn, more children, more love, or more money: it will require a seed.

The seed is the Word of God, the incorruptible seed which never returns void. Just like a farmer, if we plant nothing, then it should come as no surprise that nothing grows. But somehow, we expect God to provide an increase where no seed has been planted.

I planted, Apollos watered, but God [all the while] was causing the growth. So neither is the one who plants nor the one who waters anything, but [only] God who causes the growth.

1 Corinthians 3:6-7 (AMP)

Harvest without seed would undermine the credibility of God and would be a violation of His established principle regarding increase: seed, time, then harvest. God planted His Son and grew a Savior; Jesus was the First Fruit Seed and became the Harvest for the world.

Bring ye all the tithes into the storehouse, that there may be meat in mine house, and prove me now herewith, saith the Lord of hosts, if I will not open you the windows of heaven, and pour you out a blessing, that there shall not be room enough to receive it. Malachi 3:10

Another hindrance to receiving is the inability to believe that if you give, it will be given unto you. Subsequently, we don't trust enough to give, and our lives generally reflect that fact.

I've heard it said that when we give, we shouldn't expect anything from God because He saved us, and that should be enough. Well, God not only tells you to give, but He tells you how it will be returned to you. Pressed down, shaken together, and running over. So I encourage you to expect a harvest for every seed that you sow.

Give, and it will be given to you. A good measure, pressed down, shaken together and running over, will be poured into your lap. For with the measure you use, it will be measured to you. Luke 6:38 (NIV)

Money is the only topic in the Bible in which God asks you to trust Him with your increase. Again, He tells you how it will return to you as a harvest. He promises to open the windows of heaven and bless you beyond your ability to contain it. That's how God's economy works. The Blessing.

Trust in the Blood of Jesus is essential here because, without an understanding, you may get the wrong idea that God wants your money. No! God wants your seed because no seed equals no harvest, and that's like being a Kingdom Citizen without the benefit of the Kingdom's economy.

Trust God and sow. If you worship any place where you are reluctant to give, you need to worship elsewhere because freely giving is a beautiful part of worship. God tells us to give from the heart, and that He loves a cheerful giver. Ask Holy Spirit to direct you in your giving. Be Blessed!

Declaration: Father, thank You for continuing to reveal to me the gift of sowing. I declare that I'm a giver, and I participate by faith in the harvest made available to me through the Blood of Jesus. I sow in love, and gratitude fully expecting to see Your increase in every area of my life, in the name of Jesus. Amen.

Blood-Bought Promises Too

Day 17

Redemption

When we hear the word "redemption," there is often vagueness about what it means to the Body of Christ. The word redemption refers to the buying back of something, or, in this case, someone. Redemption literally means "repurchase" or "buyback."

We see a type of this concept illustrated in the book of Hosea, 3:1-2. Hosea was instructed by God to marry Gomer, a known prostitute, and he did what God asked. However, after marriage, she continued to cheat on him with other men and even had children from those affairs. When Gomer was about to be sold into a life of slavery because of her prostitution, God told Hosea to go and redeem her. Later, we see Hosea, the one who had been most injured by his wife's adultery, show up and pay her debt so she could escape the penalty of her failure.

That is a type and shadow or picture of what Jesus has done for us. With His blood, He redeemed us from the spiritual consequences of our failure. God has promised that our redemption is complete in Jesus Christ. God has taken the punishment that was rightfully ours and placed it on Jesus as our perfect substitute, our Redeemer.

In him we have redemption through his blood, the forgiveness of sins, in accordance with the riches of God's grace... Ephesians 1:7 (NIV)

Jesus was judged for every bad thing that we have done or will ever do. That is why Jesus stated that "it" was finished. The work of forgiveness, salvation, and oneness with God was complete. We've been redeemed!

Jesus gave his life for our sins, just as God our Father planned, in order to rescue us from this evil world in which we live. Galatians 1:4 (NLT)

What this redemption did for us was to remove all the curses (Jesus having become a curse for us) and restore us to Genesis 1:26. The Blessing. Never again do we have to lean toward superstition or the idea that God is out to get us.

In this is love, not that we loved God, but that He loved us and sent His Son to be the propitiation [that is, the atoning sacrifice, and the satisfying offering] for our sins [fulfilling God's requirement for justice against sin and placating His wrath].
1 John 4:10 (AMP)

Because of the Blood of Jesus, we are redeemed and positioned to receive all that God has made available through His promises. Agree with God and declare that Christ has redeemed you. Be Blessed!

Declaration: Father, thank You for the finished work of the Blood of Jesus. You said, "let the redeemed of the Lord say so." I declare that I'm redeemed and perfectly positioned to receive all that is mine by divine right because of the Blood of Jesus. All is well with my family and me. You perfect all that concerns me in Jesus' name, Amen.

Blood-Bought Promises Too

Day 18

Kingdom Citizenship

When we accept Christ as our Savior, we transfer from the kingdom of darkness into the kingdom of light. We relocate from a life of blindness into an abundant life, as John 10:10 tells us.

In the knowledge of Christ, we literally move from the Kingdom of the Damned to the Kingdom of the Most High. For many of us, especially in the U.S., we don't necessarily have a real understanding of the Kingdom.

So let me define it: a kingdom is a king's territory and his sovereign right to rule it. It's also defined as the king's dominion, a territory having a monarchical form of government headed by a king.

Giving thanks unto the Father, which hath made us meet to be partakers of the inheritance of the saints in light: Who hath delivered us from the power of darkness, and hath translated us into the kingdom of his dear Son. Colossians 1:12-13

Now, if you're a citizen of the kingdom, all the wealth and the resources of the kingdom are there to provide for the wellbeing of the people. The highest priority of a good king is caring for the needs of the people. Jesus is the King of kings.

But my God shall supply all your need according to his riches in glory by Christ Jesus. Philippians 4:19

As I mentioned, a kingdom is defined by its territory, and the sovereign has a right to rule it. So God, as Earth's Creator, decided that Jesus is the King of Heaven and Earth, which includes everything we see or will ever see. God owns it all; Earth, space, outer space, and all of its resources.

In the beginning, God created the heaven and the earth.
Genesis 1:1

Every good thing in this world is for citizens of the Kingdom of God, but citizenship alone wasn't enough. God wanted us in His family.

But to as many as did receive and welcome Him, He gave the right [the authority, the privilege] to become children of God, that is, to those who believe in (adhere to, trust in, and rely on) His name— John 1:12 (AMP)

Remember, the earth and its resources are the inheritance of the sons and daughters of God, the citizens of the Kingdom. The Bible says that because of the Blood of Jesus, we are now a Royal Priesthood and Kings.

But to all who believed him and accepted him, he gave the right to become children of God. John 1:12 (NLT)

...And giving joyful thanks to the Father, who has qualified you to share in the inheritance of his holy people in the kingdom of light. Colossians 1:12 (NIV)

It's interesting to note that kings aren't elected; legitimately, only blood can qualify you to be a king. So, God, through the Blood of Jesus, has elevated us, who believe, into the kingdom to partake of all the rights and privileges of a citizen, son, or daughter.

Here in America, citizens have many rights. However, the only rights that benefit anyone are the ones they are aware of and the ones they exercise.

If you don't know your rights, I promise you'll live beneath your privilege. You won't make demands because you don't know you have that right. Hosea 4:6 says, "my people perish for lack of knowledge."

Many believers have not spent enough time in our Bill Of Rights, AKA the New Covenant in Blood, to become familiar with the rights of a blood-bought citizen.

It is here that we learn that Satan has no power to govern a blood-bought believer.

We would learn that sickness, poverty, lack, even death is not a part of God's Kingdom. We would also know that God doesn't impute sin to Kingdom Citizens.

We would learn that Jesus alone is enough to move all who will believe from the kingdom of darkness into the Kingdom of Light.

Ask Holy Spirit to make you sensitive to Kingdom principles so that the Kingdom mindset develops in you.

In your life together, think the way Christ Jesus thought.
He was like God in every way,
but he did not think that his being equal with God was
something to use for his own benefit. Philippians 2:5-6 (ERV)

Do you think Jesus has a Kingdom mindset?

Do not conform to the pattern of this world, but be transformed by the renewing of your mind. Romans 12:2 (NIV)
And Be Blessed!

Declaration: Father, thank You for adoption into Your family through the Blood of Jesus. Because of Your love, I am now one with You. Thank You for access to all Your Kingdom has for its citizens. By faith, I take peace, prosperity, and wholeness in Jesus' name, Amen.

Blood-Bought Promises Too

Day 19

You Have What You Say

We as believers often forget that as speaking spirits made in the image of God, we create with our words. God demonstrated that, with His faith-filled spoken Words. He showed that creating the visible through the invisible was not only possible, but the way we're supposed to use words.

Words are for creation and blessing. The first thing God did was to create Adam and bless him in Genesis 1:1, 26.

Our words are always creating our world. However, most are unaware of the power of their words. We're continually practicing speech patterns that create situations and issues that make our lives harder than they have to be.

He who guards his mouth and his tongue Guards himself from troubles. Proverbs 21:23 (AMP)

There were times in Scripture where God caused someone to become mute in order to keep them from speaking unbelief. The things we say frame our world.

The angel said to him, "I am Gabriel. I stand in the presence of God, and I have been sent to speak to you and to tell you this good news. And now you will be silent and not able to speak until the day this happens, because you did not believe my words, which will come true at their appointed time."

Luke 1:19 (NIV)

The Bible tells us that we shall decide a thing and declare it, and it will be established.

Thou shalt also decree a thing, and it shall be established unto thee... Job 22:28

Plainly said, if you keep saying it, it will end up in your heart (spirit man). Then, the Bible says, "So as a man thinks in His spirit man, so is he," Proverbs 23:7. So the pattern becomes "we don't believe our words create," so we say everything that represents a cursed life, and then we complain to God about how hard it is.

However, when we recognize our God-like ability to create with our words, we'll begin to agree with God. You know, when God tells me I'm blessed, I agree and say that I'm blessed. God tells me I'm healed, so I say I'm healed. Why?

Because God is only bound to keep the words, He said. So the next time you're tempted to say, "If it's not one thing it's another," pause and say, "If it's not one good thing, it's another." When that unexpected bill shows up, declare that your God supplies all your needs, Philippians 4:19.

The Bible tells us that our mouths speak both blessings and curses, James 3:10; life or death, and to choose life, Deuteronomy 30:19. Whenever we decide to say what God has said, we are choosing the blessing, not the curse; we are choosing life, not death.

Death and life are in the power of the tongue, And those who love it and indulge it will eat its fruit and bear the consequences of their words. Proverbs 18:21 (AMP)

In times of stress or pressure, ask Holy Spirit to show you how to handle the situation. The Blood of Jesus has provided access to the wisdom of God in every area of life, but the result we receive will greatly depend on the words we say at the start.

Second Kings 4:8-37 talks about the Shunammite woman who woke up to find her son had died, but when her husband asked what was wrong, all she would say was, "All is well." She went out to find the Prophet Elijah because she knew he was a man of God and understood the power of the spoken word.

When she found him, he asked her if everything was okay, and she said, "All is well, but I need you to come to my home with me now."

When they returned to her home, Elijah raised the boy back to life. What is most interesting about this account is that years earlier, Elijah asked this very woman if there was anything he could go to God for on her behalf, and she said she wanted a son.

But during this crisis, she knew not to open her mouth and speak that her son was dead. She knew that it was her words, the spoken request that brought her a son, and she somehow knew to agree with God and declare that all was well even in the midst of what seemed to be a tragic situation.

Mark 11:24 says that whatever petition you make, believe you receive it, and you shall have what you say. And Be Blessed!

Declaration: Father, thank You for the power to create good with my words. Holy Spirit, help me to be sensitive to my words, teach me to speak the blessing when I'm tempted to say something negative. I decree that All Is Well with me and my words will always be a blessing in Jesus' name, Amen.

Blood-Bought Promises Too

Day 20

God Promises Angelic Interaction

Throughout the Bible, we see the mention of angels. In most instances, the angel has come as a messenger of God, such as in Luke 22:43, where God sent a spiritual messenger to strengthen Jesus before His suffering on the cross. So angels can provide strength to us when needed to accomplish the things of God; everything that was available to Christ is available to us through faith.

And there appeared an angel unto him from heaven, strengthening him. Luke 22:43

And all things that are Mine are Yours, and [all things that are] Yours are Mine… Holy Father, keep them in Your name, the name which You have given Me, so that they may be one just as We are. John 17:10-11 (AMP)

Angels also appeared to give direction at the tomb of Jesus; see Matthew 28:1-2. The angel declares to Mary Magdalene that Jesus has risen in Mark 16:5-6. He also tells them to meet in Galilee, Matthew 28:2-7. Angels also appear to the disciples and inform them that Christ will return to Earth in the same way He left.

While they were looking intently into the sky as He was going, two men in white clothing suddenly stood beside them, who said, "Men of Galilee, why do you stand looking into the sky? This [same] Jesus, who has been taken up from you into heaven, will return in just the same way as you have watched Him go into heaven." Acts 1:10-11 (AMP)

We, as believers, have a blood-bought right to expect angelic direction and information.

After Herod Agrippa imprisoned Peter, God sent an angel to free him and lead him to safety.

And, behold, the angel of the Lord came upon him, and a light shined in the prison: and he smote Peter on the side, and raised him up, saying, Arise up quickly. And his chains fell off from his hands. Acts 12:7

An angel also revealed prophecies to John, which later became the book of Revelation.

...and He sent and communicated it by His angel (divine messenger) to His bond-servant John .. Revelation 1:1 (AMP)

As we can see, throughout the New Testament, angels are present and busy facilitating the will of God; however, in Revelation 22:6-11, we are warned not to worship angels, only God. So what are the angels doing for believers today?

Revelation 14:6 says that angels proclaim the eternal gospel to those who live on Earth, to every nation, tribe, language, and people. They are trying to convince people of God's love for them through Jesus Christ.

Be Blessed!

Declaration: Father, thank You for angelic intervention in my affairs. I declare that I'm sensitive to the spiritual realm, and I hear clearly from You. I decree I receive insight, guidance, direction, and protection from every plan of the enemy. All Is Well With Me In Jesus' Name! Amen.

Blood-Bought Promises Too

Day 21

Power in the Word

It sounds a little cliché when we hear the phrase, "Power in the Word." But, if we understand that Jesus is the Word and that God and His Word are one, then it takes on a meaning that is anything but cliché.

Let's think for a moment. The Bible states that the Word created everything. Now the Word was not just who Jesus was in the flesh, but the Word was also the truth of God regarding who Jesus was and why He came into the world.

Before anything else existed, there was Christ, with God. He has always been alive and is himself God. He created everything there is—nothing exists that he didn't make. Eternal life is in him, and this life gives light to all mankind. His life is the light that shines through the darkness—and the darkness can never extinguish it. John 1:1-5 (TLB)

For God so loved the world, that he gave his only begotten Son, that whosoever believeth in him should not perish, but have everlasting life. John 3:16

In Genesis, we see God call forth the world we know with the power of His Words: *And God said, Let there be light: and there was light,* Genesis 1:3.

God also says He made us in His image and likeness, which means he created us to act like Him: *And God said, Let us make man in our image after our likeness,* Genesis 1:26.

We are to use the power of His Words to call forth and create as He would: *God, who gives life to the dead and calls into being that which does not exist,* Romans 4:17 (AMP).

He said that the entire world is held together by the Word of His Power—Hebrews 1:3.

The Bible says that we shall decide a thing and declare it, and it will be established: *Thou shalt also decree a thing, and it shall be established unto thee: and the light shall shine upon thy ways,* Job 20:28.

We are instructed to use our faith-filled words to bind and loose in the earth. Don't just let the devil run through your life, Say Something: Matthew 18:18.

The angels harken to the words of God. We have to understand that we're always giving licenses with our words. We are spirit beings, and there's more to life than meets the eye. The Army of God is waiting for your command.

Praise the Lord, you his angels, you mighty ones who do his bidding, who obey his word. Psalm 103:20 (NIV)

The words we choose to release allow access into our lives for better or worse.

But when we use God's Words, we are agreeing with God giving Him a license to operate in our situation on our behalf. When Mary was visited by an angel and found out she would be the birth mother of Jesus, her response was to agree. She said, "Be it done as you have spoken."

She permitted God to use her to bring Jesus into the earth. The power in the word is rooted in God's sovereign power and faithfulness.

God is not a man. He cannot lie. Numbers 23:19

So, no matter what needs to change in your life, find the Word from God about the issue and say what God said to unlock the power in the Word. The Word of God is the incorruptible seed and will always produce. God said His words would never return void but produce what the Bible has promised.

So shall my word be that goeth forth out of my mouth: it shall not return unto me void, but it shall accomplish that which I please, and it shall prosper in the thing whereto I sent it.

Isaiah 55:11

Everything God has said to us has been a promise simply because He cannot lie. Furthermore, Jesus has qualified every believer through His blood to operate in the power of the Word in faith.

Because of the Blood of Jesus. Whenever we trust the promises of God, the answer to every promise is yes when we agree with our spoken amen. Agree with God today about what He has said. You are blessed and highly favored; you are the righteousness of God in Christ. You are healed and anointed to do good works.

For as many as are the promises of God, in Christ they are [all answered] "Yes." So through Him we say our "Amen" to the glory of God. 2 Corinthians 1:20(AMP)

Ask Holy Spirit to help you to respond with the Word of God no matter what you're facing. Speak the result you want to see, not what you're feeling at that moment. And Be Blessed!

Blood-Bought Promises Too

Day 22

Emotional Healing/Broken-Hearted

Emotions play such a large part in how our lives progress, and unfortunately, for some, our hearts have often been injured or flat out broken. For most people, we heal over time and go on with our lives, maybe a little more cautious and perhaps more cynical, but we move on.

But for some of us, this broken-heartedness is paralyzing, and we're stuck in that time, in that space. This is a trick to stop your assignment; this is not the will of God. No matter what has broken your heart, you must know that first, God is not responsible for the events that led to the heartbreak. Secondly, Jesus Himself says that His assignment and His anointing is to heal the brokenhearted.

The Spirit of the Lord is upon me, because he hath anointed me to preach the gospel to the poor; he hath sent me to heal the brokenhearted, to preach deliverance to the captives, and recovering of sight to the blind, to set at liberty them that are bruised... Luke 4:18

We have to be aware that our feelings are often the result of what we are thinking. So for many of us, it would be best if we stop playing over and over the video in our heads. Redirecting our attention from our hurt to the promises of God will produce different emotions; your faith will grow, and your expectations will change. God, your Father, wants to restore your joy and redeem the time you spent trapped in heartbreak.

He heals the brokenhearted And binds up their wounds [healing their pain and comforting their sorrow].
Psalm 147:3 (AMP)

Ask Holy Spirit to direct you in taking steps to get beyond whatever has attempted to rob you of God's best. Your purpose will go unmet if you allow the hurt to stop you in your tracks.

Allow the Word of God to bring light in the dark spaces. It is His will that you live an abundant life, and through the Blood of Jesus, He has made healing for broken-heartedness available in Christ.

The Lord is close to the brokenhearted; he rescues those whose spirits are crushed. Psalm 34:18 (NLT)

Satan has no right to your future or your emotions regardless of the circumstances.

Allow God to lead you to peace beyond understanding through the knowledge of Jesus. You will find that the joy of the Lord will provide strength to not only conquer heartbreak but also to fulfill your God-given purpose. Be Blessed!

Declaration: Father, thank You for Your great love for me. Thank You for the Blood of Jesus, which removed all barriers to Your restoration. I declare that all is well with me, and I look forward to the abundant life You've planned for me. Holy Spirit, lead and guide me in my thinking and emotions. Remind me of God's promises whenever I'm tempted to look at the past hurt. I am blessed and highly favored by God, in Jesus' name, Amen.

Blood-Bought Promises Too

Day 23

Freedom from a Guilty Mind

As believers, we often forget that even when we sin or miss the mark, we must quickly remind ourselves that we are the righteousness of God in Christ Jesus. It's important to remember that truth even when we come up short of God's best. Although our actions have consequences, our righteousness before God is not based on our activities, good or bad. The believer's righteousness is based on faith in the work of the Blood of Jesus.

For we maintain that an individual is justified by faith distinctly apart from works of the Law [the observance of which has nothing to do with justification, that is, being declared free of the guilt of sin and made acceptable to God].

Romans 3:28 (AMP)

Now, that's in no way a license to live a life of disobedience to God. On the contrary, we should continuously be increasing our dependency on Holy Spirit's guidance to walk on God's prepared path. However, when we fail, we have assurance through the blood that we are forgiven. This truth is essential to remember, especially when we think we've done something that should make God abandon us in our failure.

In whom we have redemption through his blood, the forgiveness of sins, according to the riches of his grace...

Ephesians 1:7

...Yet we know that a man is not justified [and placed in right standing with God] by works of the Law, but [only] through faith in [God's beloved Son,] Christ Jesus. By observing the Law no one will ever be justified [declared free of the guilt of sin and its penalty]. Galatians 2:16 (AMP)

This word "forgiven" has often been undervalued and held without much regard by many religious leaders as to its full weight. Forgiven has been defined as the act of pardoning someone, but it also means to forget as though it never happened. Now, that's pretty heavy considering our usual approach of, "Well, I'll forgive, but I won't forget."

One example of this is in the book of Hebrews, chapter 10, where God demonstrates true forgiveness when He tells us that He forgives us and our transgressions; sins and iniquities He will remember no more. God has no memory of a believer's sins and keeps no record because of the Blood of Jesus.

For I will be merciful to their unrighteousness, and their sins and their iniquities will I remember no more. Hebrews 8:12

God has promised not to remember every time you miss the mark, and you have to do the same. Let's not forget we have an adversary who is only too happy to replay your sin failures and constantly remind you that you have failed.

He'll lie to you and tell you that God is angry with you, and He can never bless or help you now because you're a sinner, and God doesn't hear sinners. The devil is a liar! Believers aren't sinners; we're saints because of the blood.

Satan is the accuser of the brethren, and he wants to rob you of confidence in the promises of God. He wants to create guilt and condemnation because it will directly attack your faith. Guilt is not of God, and part of the work of the cross was to purge us of fear, a guilty conscience, and the constant mindset of unworthiness. Hallelujah! The Blood of Jesus has made you worthy.

Let us go right into the presence of God with sincere hearts fully trusting him. For our guilty consciences have been sprinkled with Christ's blood to make us clean...

Hebrews 10:22a (NLT)

The Blood of Jesus has made the vertical relationship between our spirit and God perfect in Christ. However, when we know that something we've done has negatively affected someone, we should feel a tugging at our core to address the matter with direction from Holy Spirit. We should never feel condemned, but we should be sensitive to the spirit and the feelings of others.

Therefore there is now no condemnation [no guilty verdict, no punishment] for those who are in Christ Jesus [who believe in Him as personal Lord and Savior]. Romans 8:1 (AMP)

Sometimes forgiving ourselves is the hardest part. However, Holy Spirit wants you whole, so He'll show you how to redirect your thoughts to the love and acceptance of God. Ask Him to show you how to reconcile with any injured party and follow His prompting. It's been my experience that when we have offended someone, we typically know what we should do to repair the offense, but often our pride prevents us from taking action.

I pray that you follow the prompting of Holy Spirit to resolve any issue that causes you to feel guilty. As far as God is concerned, you are free from condemnation and guilt through the Blood of Jesus. It is important to understand that everyone does not forgive like God, but do the part you can as directed by Holy Spirit.

But when he, the Spirit of truth, comes, he will guide you into all the truth. John 16:13 (NIV)

No matter what you are dealing with today, ask Holy Spirit to give you step-by-step actions to resolve the root of the guilt. Don't allow guilt consciousness to put space between you and God; it's a trick of Satan. The Blood of Jesus has removed all barriers to God for the believer. You have a blood-bought right to have the peace and assurance promised by Jesus at the center of your consciousness. Be Blessed!

Declaration: Father, thank You for a sound mind free of guilt and condemnation. I thank You for the Blood of Jesus that has removed every hint of shame or unworthiness from my thinking. I am the righteousness of God in Christ Jesus. I decree that I grow in the understanding of Your love for me daily. I am led into all truth by Your Holy Spirit in Jesus' name, Amen.

Blood-Bought Promises Too

Day 24

Authority

Many believers think that God alone is responsible for the lives we live and every situation we find ourselves in, but they fail to grasp the fact that God has given man the legal right to exercise authority in the earth. We often suffer as we wait for God to step in when the Bible tells us that we must lay hands on the sick, we must cast out the demons, we must decree and declare a thing for it to be established or implemented.

And these signs shall follow them that believe; In my name shall they cast out devils; they shall speak with new tongues; They shall take up serpents; and if they drink any deadly thing, it shall not hurt them; they shall lay hands on the sick, and they shall recover. Mark 16:17-18

Jesus demonstrated His authority and control over natural elements as the Son of Man. He told the storm to stop, and it obeyed. He didn't ask God to stop the wind; Jesus commanded it to stop.

Then God said, "Let Us (Father, Son, Holy Spirit) make man in Our image, according to Our likeness [not physical, but a spiritual personality and moral likeness]; and let them have complete authority over the fish of the sea, the birds of the air, the cattle, and over the entire earth, and over everything that creeps and crawls on the earth." Genesis 1:26 (AMP)

Question: If God is in absolute control of every event that takes place in the lives of everything created, then how would it be possible to command a storm that God ordained to be there to stop? Jesus put it this way: *And the Lord said, If ye had faith as a grain of mustard seed, ye might say unto this sycamine tree, Be thou plucked up by the root, and be thou planted in the sea; and it should obey you*, in Luke 17:6.

For verily I say unto you, That whosoever shall say unto this mountain, Be thou removed, and be thou cast into the sea; and shall not doubt in his heart, but shall believe that those things which he saith shall come to pass; he shall have whatsoever he saith. Mark 11:23

If you have faith, you can command that mountain into the sea. He did not say if you pray and ask God to move the mountain, He "might." Much of what we are waiting on God to do He has already done; now He's waiting for us to operate in the authority He gave to man in Genesis 1:26.

But just like the children of Israel, we refuse to enter or operate in our God-given authority because of unbelief. God believes in us, and He has trusted us with His dominion and control over the earth for a set time period. This authority is part of what the blood of Jesus came to restore to humanity after the fall of Adam.

God desires that believers be co-heirs and co-laborers with Christ, and that means we operate in the authority of God. He's even given us the Name of Jesus to use to ensure His will goes forth. He has deposited His Holy Spirit in us to lead and guide us in the proper use of this authority.

When I hear people say that God is in control, I think to myself, He most certainly is but probably not in the way you're thinking. God is sovereign, and God is in charge, but as with anyone in control, God did what He wanted, how He wanted, and He decided to allow us to rule the earth with His guidance.

We have the responsibility of stewardship over the earth; that means we have the authority to advance God's agenda. When we encounter things in the world, our atmosphere, or our lives that don't line up with the will of God, we have the right and the obligation to use the Word of God and the name of Jesus to change that situation.

Poverty, sickness, depression, strife, and hatred are not of God, but He's not coming down from heaven to do what He has authorized us to do with the name of Jesus.

And whatsoever ye shall ask in my name, that will I do, that the Father may be glorified in the Son. If ye shall ask any thing in my name, I will do it. John 14:13-14

We've been on the sidelines waiting for God to do our part for too long. You don't have to tolerate the harassment of the devil in any area of your life. God is waiting for us to take our rightful place of authority through the Blood of Jesus. When we say what God has said, we're operating in the authority of His Word. Be Blessed!

Thou shalt also decree a thing, and it shall be established unto thee: and the light shall shine upon thy ways. Job 22:28

Declaration: Father, thank You for the wisdom to operate in your authority. Thank You for Your guidance and direction. Holy Spirit, teach me to be sensitive to areas where I need to exercise my blood-bought authority to decree the Word of God over situations that oppose the will of God for my life. I decree that all is well with me, and I'm led by Your Holy Spirit, in Jesus' name, Amen.

Blood-Bought Promises Too

Day 25

Reconciliation

When we look at the word "reconciliation," it's considered an accounting term that means to harmonize or to bring into alignment. It means to change or exchange. It also means to bring together two parties that have been enemies into a relationship of peace or to reunite.

We must get this because that is what Jesus did through His blood for every believer. He changed the nature of the relationship between God and man. Before Jesus shed His blood, we were spiritual enemies of God.

For if while we were enemies we were reconciled to God through the death of His Son, it is much more certain, having been reconciled, that we will be saved [from the consequences of sin] by His life [that is, we will be saved because Christ lives today]. Not only that, but we also rejoice in God [rejoicing in His love and perfection] through our Lord Jesus Christ, through whom we have now received and enjoy our reconciliation [with God]. Romans 5:10-11 (AMP)

And all things are of God, who hath reconciled us to himself by Jesus Christ, and hath given to us the ministry of reconciliation... 2 Corinthians 5:18

Now, because of the death, burial, and resurrection of Jesus, our relationship is positioned to be in harmony with

God again. Our debt is paid, and as far as God is concerned, you have a zero sin balance. God accepted Christ's payment and applied it to your account. The books are balanced, and all believers are reconciled in Christ.

However, as believers, we must accept the gift of reconciliation that Jesus has made available by agreeing with the Word of God by faith. For us to continue to believe that there is any barrier between God and us after accepting Jesus is not biblical. Ask Holy Spirit to help you in understanding that God is not mad at you, Jesus positioned you for favor and the blessing of the Lord; receive! Be Blessed!

Therefore, since we have been justified [that is, acquitted of sin, declared blameless before God] by faith, [let us grasp the fact that] we have peace with God [and the joy of reconciliation with Him] through our Lord Jesus Christ (the Messiah, the Anointed). Romans 5:1 (AMP)

Colossians 1:19: *For it pleased the Father that in him should all fullness dwell; And, having made peace through the blood of his cross, by him to reconcile all things unto himself; by him, I say, whether they be things in earth, or things in heaven. And you, that were sometime alienated and enemies in your mind by wicked works, yet now hath he reconciled.*

Declaration: Thank You, Father, for reconciliation through the Blood of Jesus. Because of the blood, I am the righteousness of God in Christ, and no good thing will You withhold from me. Because of Your great love for me, You have given me these promises in Your Word, and You cannot lie. I receive and agree with them by faith, and I give Holy Spirit authority to establish them in my heart and mind in Jesus' name, Amen.

Blood-Bought Promises Too

Day 26

Fearless

Fear seems to be the prevailing sentiment in our society these days. Everywhere we go, there is someone who reminds us to be afraid. When we turn on our televisions, we are bombarded with news that reminds us to fear. Many of us during church attendance are served up a steady diet of fear, which is strange because, as believers, we are cautioned not to be afraid and not operate in fear.

Fear is a negative emotion that, if left unchecked, will make our minds unstable and destroy the faith necessary to enjoy the things God has made available through the Blood of Jesus. Fear is not of God.

There is no fear in love. But perfect love drives out fear, because fear has to do with punishment. The one who fears is not made perfect in love. 1 John 4:18 (NIV)

The Bible tells us in 2 Timothy that God did not give us the spirit of fear. Therefore, one of the first things we must do whenever fear, or worry for that matter, comes upon us, we have to remember, this is not God!

For God hath not given us the spirit of fear; but of power, and of love, and of a sound mind. 2 Timothy 1:7

Now, I think most of us would confess that the majority of

things that we fear and worry about never actually happen. So what does the spirit of fear produce? It serves to undermine your faith in God's promises. It distracts us from hearing from God when we focus on the worst possible outcome.

You see, that's what fear does: it focuses our attention on the worst possible outcome instead of the Word of God. The second part of 2 Timothy1:7 states, "but instead a sound mind." So we can see from the Scripture that the spirit of fear is the enemy of a sound mind. Why? Because God wants us to keep our minds entirely focused on what He has promised. That's not possible if we are in fear and negative meditation. Replace fear, doubt, and worry with the promises of God: faith comes by hearing the Word of God.

That's what fear and worry are: they're a form of negative meditation. But the Word tells us that we will be in perfect peace when we meditate on Jesus and the Good News of the Gospel.

Thou wilt keep him in perfect peace, whose mind is stayed on thee: because he trusteth in thee. Trust ye in the Lord for ever: for in the Lord Jehovah is everlasting strength...

Isaiah 26:3-4

Fear is an enemy to faith, so no matter what you fear today, bind it in the name of Jesus and declare the peace of the Lord. Ask Holy Spirit to lead you regarding the spirit of fear with step-by-step instructions to overcome anything that threatens your peace.

Our emotions, good or bad, tend to follow our thoughts. So, when you have an idea that says you'll never please God, remember that as Christ is, so are we in this world. Declare "I am the righteousness of God in Christ." If God is pleased with Christ, then God is pleased with me. Christ is my substitute, and my identity is in Christ.

Herein is our love made perfect, that we may have boldness in the day of judgment: because as he is, so are we in this world.

1 John 4:17

If you fear that you can't make it financially, remember to declare that "God supplies all my needs according to his riches in glory by Christ Jesus," Philippians 4:19.

If you've received a bad medical report, remember that you are already healed. By His stripes, you *were* healed—past tense, Isaiah 53:5.

The point here is that our emotions typically go in the direction of our thoughts, and our words will generally follow our feelings. So here is the pattern: thoughts, feelings, words, then actions.

When we get our thoughts locked in on the promises of God, it will change how we feel. When we feel different, we speak and act differently. We must renew our minds daily because life gives us daily opportunities to be directed by the spirit of fear. Be Blessed!

For as he thinketh in his heart, so is he... Proverbs 23:7

Declaration: Father, thank You for fearlessness. I decree that You perfect everything that concerns me. I don't fear because You are with me. Holy Spirit, thank You for leading and guiding me in my thought life. All is well with me, and You, Father, supply everything I need. I am never without what I need, and You will never allow me to be put to shame. I have favor with You and everyone I come in contact with, in Jesus' name, Amen.

Blood-Bought Promises Too

Day 27

Faith

When we hear the term "faith," we often think of this element of the Christian life that's abstract or perhaps even unmeasurable. But, understanding faith is too important to leave in a gray area. As stated in the Word, our salvation comes by grace but through faith.

For by grace are ye saved through faith; and that not of yourselves: it is the gift of God... Ephesians 2:8-9

The Bible tells us in Hebrews 11:6 that without faith, it is impossible to please God. It also states that with faith, all things are possible in Mark 9:23.

I've heard people say, "I wish I had more faith," but the truth is, the only way to get more faith is to get more Word because faith comes by hearing the Word of God.

Faith, like everything else that God offers, is a gift available by His grace through our faith in the Blood of Jesus. God has given every man the measure of faith, which means He gave everyone the same "faith seed."

"According as God hath dealt to every man the measure of faith." Romans 12:3

Our responsibility is to grow it by hearing the Word of God. Therefore, when we hear the gospel preached, it must be mixed with the faith seed that God provides to manifest the promise in the Bible.

For unto us was the gospel preached, as well as unto them: but the word preached did not profit them, not being mixed with faith in them that heard it. Hebrews 4:2

But as Jesus said, "Faith without works is dead," James 2:20. Now don't get too religious here. I'm not talking about works to get God to do something. I'm talking about corresponding actions that manifest what God has already made available to those who would believe. Below is an illustration of faith in action.

"While I am in the world, I am the light of the world." After Jesus said this, he spit on the dirt, made some mud and put it on the man's eyes. Jesus told him, "Go and wash in Siloam pool." (Siloam means "Sent.") So the man went to the pool, washed and came back. He was now able to see. John 9:5-7 (ERV)

This man would never have received healing had he not believed Jesus enough to act on what he heard. This is a beautiful picture of faith. He heard and agreed with God, and the promise of sight was manifested. His faith in action made him whole.

Just as a farmer has to believe that the soil will return a harvest after he has planted his seeds, we have to believe the Word of God before we will act. We live in a voice-activated world, so when we hear instructions from God, we must start by agreeing with God.

Now, if you have faith and trust in God's promises, then just like the farmer and the blind man, you will act on what you believe and sow the seed.

This is the picture of our faith in action. Here is God's system: faith takes hold of what God's grace has made available through the Blood of Jesus.

Jesus replied, "Have faith in God [constantly]. I assure you and most solemnly say to you, whoever says to this mountain, 'Be lifted up and thrown into the sea!' and does not doubt in his heart [in God's unlimited power], but believes that what he says is going to take place, it will be done for him [in accordance with God's will]. For this reason I am telling you, whatever things you ask for in prayer [in accordance with God's will], believe [with confident trust] that you have received them, and they will be given to you." Mark 11:22-24 (AMP)

Whenever you're tempted to believe that your faith is insufficient, keep in mind that the faith you're using came directly from God and produces God's results. The Bible tells us that every promise of God is "yea and amen" in Christ. If you've accepted Christ as your savior, you have a blood-bought right to see the promises of God manifest in your circumstances and situations.

If you want to increase your faith, spend more time with the Word of God, and watch your faith explode. Faith in God is the result of hearing the Word of God. Be Blessed!

Declaration: Father God, thank You for the gift of faith. Holy Spirit, direct me in my faith walk as I grow in the manifestation of the promises of God. Your presence makes me sensitive to any areas where I've not allowed my faith to develop. I bind any thoughts that attempt to limit my growth, and I decree all is well in Jesus' name. Amen.

Blood-Bought Promises Too

Day 28

Healing

When it comes to healing, we as believers must start any conversation with some foundational Scriptures. By His stripes, we were healed.

Who his own self bare our sins in his own body on the tree, that we, being dead to sins, should live unto righteousness: by whose stripes ye were healed. 1 Peter 2:24 (KJV)

It's clear that this Scripture is past tense, which means that it's already done. Now, this is when our faith has to be applied to our situation.

The Bible states in Matthew 8:17 that Christ was beaten and carried our sin on the cross for the healing of our sickness and diseases, but we have to believe that genuinely. I think it's important to note here that God does not cause disease, and the Blood of Jesus has removed every obstacle to our healing, including sin.

But it is from Him that you are in Christ Jesus, who became to us wisdom from God [revealing His plan of salvation], and righteousness [making us acceptable to God], and sanctification [making us holy and setting us apart for God], and redemption [providing our ransom from the penalty for sin]...

1 Corinthians 1:30 (AMP)

Remember, it's not our goodness or righteousness that qualifies us for healing; it's the goodness of our substitute—the Lamb of God, Jesus Christ.

We can now come boldly to the Throne of Grace with His promise in our mouth and His faith in our hearts.

Sickness is a part of the curse, and Christ came to deliver us from the curse of the law. We now live in the Blessing of the Lord.

Christ purchased our freedom and redeemed us from the curse of the Law and its condemnation by becoming a curse for us... Galatians 3:13 (AMP)

No matter what we have done, we must remember it is God's will that we prosper and be in good health, 3 John 2. Illness is one of Satan's most potent weapons. Ask Holy Spirit to lead and guide you to the Scriptures that will build your faith and manifest the healing paid for by the Blood of Jesus. It's not your worthiness that qualifies you for recovery and restoration; it's faith in the Blood of Jesus and the finished work of the cross that qualifies all believers. Be Blessed!

Declaration: Father, thank You for the gift of healing and the finished work of the cross. I decree that because of the stripes suffered by Jesus; I am healed according to the Word. Holy Spirit, help me keep my faith activated until the manifestation of my complete recovery. I declare that no weapon formed shall prosper against me. I command every part of my body to perform exactly as God designed it to function. All is well with my body, and my attitude is gratitude in Jesus' name, Amen.

Blood-Bought Promises Too

Day 29

Hope

Hope does not just wish blindly for a good outcome. Hope is the assurance of a good result because of what you know about Jesus. When you truly understand what Christ has done for us, it produces hope and the expectation of God's favor. We serve the God of hope, and His promises are the source of all real hope for the believer.

May the God of hope fill you with all joy and peace in believing [through the experience of your faith] that by the power of the Holy Spirit you will abound in hope and overflow with confidence in His promises. Romans 15:13 (AMP)

It's very reassuring to know that God is not capable of lying to us. Everything He has spoken in His Word is truth and can be relied upon to come to pass. So when we read that His grace saves us through faith, we know we are forgiven, righteous, and can now do all things through Christ if we believe.

God is not a man, that he should lie; neither the son of man, that he should repent: hath he said, and shall he not do it? or hath he spoken, and shall he not make it good? Numbers 23:19

Many of us find ourselves in what seems to be hopeless situations, but the truth is how we view and respond to concerns has a lot to do with their outcomes. Sometimes we're tempted to react to negative situations like a person with no hope, but as believers, our hope is always in Jesus. When we remember that nothing is impossible to God, it reminds us to expect good regardless of how things appear.

For with God nothing [is or ever] shall be impossible.
                                                   Luke 1:37 (AMP)

It's crucial to ask Holy Spirit to help you remain in a state of high expectation for the favor of God. God has no desire to put off the fulfillment of your hope to some later time; Christ died so you could live the abundant life now, not just in the sweet bye and bye. Hold on to your hope. Put a faith demand on the promises of God by believing and expecting to see your God-given hopes manifested.

Hope deferred makes the heart sick, But when desire is fulfilled, it is a tree of life. Proverbs 13:12 (AMP)

A promise is only as good as the one who makes it. So when we hope in what God has said, it builds faith and keeps us spiritually and mentally in the right position to see our hopes become our realities.

In this voice-activated world, it is important to say what God has said about you and your situation. There is hope in the Word of God. There is instruction for every problem that might attack your hope. As believers, our hope is built on the Blood of Jesus and His work on the cross. Expect God's best, and you will live in the promises of a Father who cannot lie. Be Blessed!

Declaration: Father, thank You for the gift of hope in Your Word. I declare that every desire that You have put in my heart will come to pass. I decree that my hope and expectation is in Jesus as both the author and finisher of my faith. I declare that Holy Spirit leads and directs me in every area of my expectations and hopes. All is well with me in Jesus' name, Amen.

Blood-Bought Promises Too

Day 30

All Sufficiency

I think it's safe to say the majority of our time is spent in search of the things we believe we need to survive and live comfortable lives. Now, there's nothing wrong with trying to provide for your family and your future, but if we attempt to do this independent of God, we often find ourselves burnt out and depleted. This idea of being self-made is a deception when it comes to believers; we must trust God and not lean on our limited understanding. The Bible states that we only exist because of God, so what about self-sufficiency?

For in Him we live and move and exist [that is, in Him we actually have our being].... Acts 17:28 (AMP)

The truth is we can't be sufficient in ourselves. God designed us for relationship and dependency on Him and the resources He's made available. When we align our thinking with God's, we gain access to what is stored up for us in Christ. God never waits for a need or issue to arise to provide what is needed. He's never late and never surprised by our circumstances, and He promises to give us all the good.

For the Lord God is a sun and shield: the Lord will give grace and glory: no good thing will he withhold from them that walk uprightly. Psalm 84:11

The Bible says that God has placed everything in Christ, and as we grow in our knowledge of Jesus and His finished work, we gain the faith to appropriate what God's grace has provided.

For His divine power has bestowed on us [absolutely] everything necessary for [a dynamic spiritual] life and godliness, through the true and personal knowledge of Him who called us by His own glory and excellence. 2 Peter 1:3 (AMP)

There is no lack in God, and He wants to make a marvelous testimony of your life by providing everything you need to demonstrate His goodness and love publicly as our Father.

So if you sinful people know how to give good gifts to your children, how much more will your heavenly Father give good gifts to those who ask him? Matthew 7:11 (NLT)

One of the keys is to ask because asking denotes our belief in His resources and His desire to provide what we ask for. Our asking demonstrates our dependency and trust in His Word. In Hebrews, we learn how to do this.

Therefore let us [with privilege] approach the throne of grace [that is, the throne of God's gracious favor] with confidence and without fear, so that we may receive mercy [for our failures] and find [His amazing] grace to help in time of need [an appropriate blessing, coming just at the right moment]. Hebrews 4:16 (AMP)

God wants us to approach His supply with boldness because, in Christ, we have the advantage of faith in His work on the cross. We come confidently and put a faith demand on the sufficiency of God because of the righteousness provided by the Blood of Jesus.

We have a blood-bought right to expect God's best in every situation. We no longer have to doubt if God will do what He's promised in His Word because we missed the mark or sinned. In Christ, we're righteous, forgiven, blessed, and positioned to receive from His supply.

For as many as are the promises of God, in Christ they are [all answered] "Yes." So through Him we say our "Amen" to the glory of God. 2 Corinthians 1:20 (AMP)

The Bible is clear that we can now come before God with confidence because of what Christ has done. We no longer depend on our efforts alone, but now in Christ, we are led by Holy Spirit to the supply made available by God.

Such is the confidence and steadfast reliance and absolute trust that we have through Christ toward God. Not that we are sufficiently qualified in ourselves to claim anything as coming from us, but our sufficiency and qualifications come from God. He has qualified us [making us sufficient] as ministers of a new covenant [of salvation through Christ], not of the letter [of a written code] but of the Spirit; for the letter [of the Law] kills [by revealing sin and demanding obedience], but the Spirit gives life. 2 Corinthians 3:4-6 (AMP)

God has qualified every believer in Christ to receive everything God has provisioned for His children. In Christ, we are forgiven, righteous, and holy before God. We are now positioned to receive all that is ours by divine right through the blood and body of Jesus. Be Blessed!

And God is able to make all grace [every favor and earthly blessing] come in abundance to you, so that you may always [under all circumstances, regardless of the need] have complete sufficiency in everything [being completely self-sufficient in Him], and have an abundance for every good work and act of charity. 2 Corinthians 9:8 (AMP)

Declaration: Father, thank You for providing everything I need for an abundant life in Christ Jesus. I declare that I am free from lack, and I have more than enough to meet my needs and to be a blessing to others. Holy Spirit, help me to keep my mind on the sufficiency of God whenever I'm tempted to focus on what I don't have. I decree that I will never be without what I need because there is no lack in Jesus. I am led and directed by Holy Spirit to the provisions for all my needs. I can do all things through Christ. I am a blessing distribution center, in Jesus' name, Amen.

Bonus
Blood-Bought Promises Too

Communion Worship

Communion is one of the most misunderstood mandates in the Christian faith. Unfortunately, because of that misunderstanding, many believers abstain and forego the benefits promised in the Bible. For many generations, believers have read to examine themselves, and I've often wondered what this self-examination would reveal about each of us. I'd imagine none would be found righteous by God's standard.

...since all have sinned and continually fall short of the glory of God... Romans 3:23 (AMP)

The Word we read here as "fall" is emphasized by the idea that this is something that happens continually. So, if only those who have not sinned according to God's standard of perfection are allowed to celebrate Jesus with communion worship, then no one would qualify.

The Scripture is clear: "Unless you eat my flesh and drink my blood, you have no life in you," John 6:53. But as believers, we are one with Christ, so communion is our worship in remembrance that Jesus took the punishment for our sin and gave us everlasting life.

Verily, verily, I say unto you, He that believeth on me hath everlasting life. John 6:47

He that eateth my flesh, and drinketh my blood, dwelleth in me, and I in Him. John 6:56

It is faith in this truth that makes believers righteous before God.

But it is from Him that you are in Christ Jesus, who became to us wisdom from God [revealing His plan of salvation], and righteousness [making us acceptable to God], and sanctification [making us holy and setting us apart for God], and redemption [providing our ransom from the penalty for sin]...
1 Corinthians 1:30 (AMP)

The righteousness of any believer is based on what Jesus has done. No person is without sin, and if there was such a person other than Christ, then the sacrifice of Jesus was unnecessary. For anyone to declare themselves righteous enough to participate in communion worship based on their behavior is an insult to God and a self-deception.

If we say that we have no sin, we deceive ourselves, and the truth is not in us. 1 John 1:8 (KJV)

So, clearly, Jesus wanted every believer to benefit from being in Him. He wanted us to eat His flesh (bread) and drink His blood (juice/wine) because both have extraordinary spiritual and physical significance.

Our redemption, forgiveness, righteousness, and holiness are the result of the Blood of Jesus. He paid the ultimate price of bearing the punishment for the sins of the entire world, for all time.

He went once for all into the Holy Place [the Holy of Holies of heaven, into the presence of God], and not through the blood of goats and calves, but through His own blood, having obtained and secured eternal redemption [that is, the salvation of all who personally believe in Him as Savior]. Hebrews 9:12 (AMP)

The Blood of Jesus has removed the sin debt for those who believe in His death, burial, and resurrection as proof that He is Lord and Savior. This is what a believer should be focused on during communion worship; Paul called it the cup of the blessing in 1 Corinthians 10. Did you get that? The blessing came by way of His blood. When we abstain from communion worship, it's like rejecting the sacrifice Jesus made to reconcile us to God. Communion worship celebrates what the blood has done to remove our sin debt, and positions us in Christ.

The Bible says that we are beneficiaries of a covenant between God the Father and God the Son. A part of that covenant included Jesus paying for the sins of the world and God accepting the blood offering as payment in full. God was fully satisfied, and He declared that the sins of man He would remember no more.

But this man, after he had offered one sacrifice for sins for ever, sat down on the right hand of God;

From henceforth expecting till his enemies be made his footstool.

For by one offering he hath perfected for ever them that are sanctified.

Whereof the Holy Ghost also is a witness to us: for after that he had said before,

This is the covenant that I will make with them after those days, saith the Lord, I will put my laws into their hearts, and in their minds will I write them;

And their sins and iniquities will I remember no more.

Now where remission of these is, there is no more offering for sin.

Having therefore, brethren, boldness to enter into the holiest by the blood of Jesus... Hebrews 10 12-19

This is such an important point that I've taken the liberty to show these passages in the (ERV), Easy To Read Version, below because this is the covenant that born-again believers should currently be operating under. When you accepted Christ, forgiveness for your sins and reconciliation with God was part of their covenant.

With one sacrifice Christ made believers spiritually perfect forever. They are the ones who are being made holy.

The Holy Spirit also tells us about this. First, He says,

"This is the agreement I will make with my people in the future," says the Lord. "I will put my laws in their hearts. I will write my laws in their minds." Then he says, "I will forget their sins and never again remember the evil they have done." And after everything is forgiven, there is no more need for a sacrifice to pay for sins.

And so, brothers and sisters, we are completely free to enter the Most Holy Place. We can do this without fear because of the blood sacrifice of Jesus. We enter through a new way that Jesus opened for us. It is a living way that leads through the curtain— Christ's body. And we have a great priest who rules the house of God. Sprinkled with the blood of Christ, our hearts have been made free from a guilty conscience, and our bodies have been washed with pure water. So come near to God with a sincere heart, full of confidence because of our faith in Christ. We must hold on to the hope we have, never hesitating to tell people about it. We can trust God to do what he promised.

Hebrews 10:14-23 (ERV)

What would be the purpose of a perfect person to participate in communion worship? The Blood of Jesus is for those of us who have missed the mark and flat out failed at keeping God's standard.

However, it provides no benefit to those worthy by perfection. Jesus came to save those who recognize they aren't perfect, and they can't keep all 613 commandments. People who know they're a work in progress, nowhere near perfect in their behavior. People who realize they need a Savior.

But if imperfection is a disqualifier and if the Blood of Jesus somehow didn't make us righteous as the Bible states, then abstaining may be wise.

But if Jesus' prayer was answered in John 17:21, then you're one with God in Christ. You have God's Holy Spirit living in you right now, so how could you possibly eat and drink unworthily?

If you're a believer who loves and reverences God and you've missed the mark and sinned in some area, this does not disqualify you from receiving communion. Communion is a celebration of Jesus hitting the mark on your behalf, and He qualifies all believers.

Our faith in the fact that He perfectly kept every rule as our substitute positions us to come to communion worship with hearts filled with gratitude, not fear and condemnation.

I want to be very clear. Sin actions will have consequences that are unpleasant and counter-productive to God's plan for our lives. These sin-traps are designed to move us away from the promises of God and to keep believers in a state of perpetual doubt about our relationship with God.

I want to assure you that your bad decisions don't render God's plan of redemption null and void. The Bible states, "where sin abounds grace abounds more," Romans 5:20, meaning God's resolution to sin is greater than your ability to sin; the offering was greater than the trespasses.

Simply put, the Blood of Jesus is greater than any sin. There are always natural repercussions for disregarding the wisdom of God, but unworthiness is not one of them. Jesus makes us worthy.

We have to reconcile ourselves to the fact that God has decided, and His choice was forgiveness for sin through belief in Jesus Christ as our sin offering.

So, if you believe that Jesus is the Savior of the world, the Lamb slain for the sins of all humanity, the resurrected Christ seated at the right hand of the Father, then worship Jesus with communion as often as possible.

There is no set time to have communion worship, just as there is no set time to pray or read the Bible. The Word says, "as often as you do this do so in remembrance" of Him, 1 Corinthians 11:24. Believe it or not, every Christian came to God the same way, needing forgiveness through Christ. Now that you've obtained it, bless the communion and worship Jesus, remembering all He endured to make that moment possible. No clergy or unique title is necessary; acknowledge that His blood has washed away your sin, and His body paid for your healing and wholeness, thank God, and partake.

God is no respecter of persons, Romans 2:11. What He's made available to one believer is open to all believers. Child of God, please don't abstain because you have misunderstood how one is qualified to partake.

It is Christ and Christ alone who makes you worthy to be in the presence of God free from the guilt and punishment for sin. Communion worship is the believer's authentication and ratification; it proclaims that what God has said about Jesus Christ is the truth; I believe it and agree. I'm Righteous by Grace through faith in Jesus The Christ.

I Love You, Be Blessed!

Blood-Bought Promises Too

Final Words

I pray that this book has been a blessing to you in some way. We're not Bible scholars, just students of the Word of God in love with Jesus. It is our deepest desire to share the Word of God in its purest form so it can be understood and implemented in our everyday lives. The Word was given so that we can carry out God's agenda on Earth. But not understanding what the Word is saying is a significant hindrance to seeing the things God has promised to manifest in our lives.

I once heard a man say that it is evidence that defeats doubt. That's why Jesus did so many miracles; it was evidence that He was who He said He was. What evidence do we as believers have that we are who we say we are if we continue to live lives full of condemnation, worry, and defeat?

The Word of God is supposed to create the evidence necessary to convince the world that He is who He says He is, and you are who He said you are: Righteous, Forgiven, Holy, Sanctified, and Anointed to do great things for the Kingdom of God.

Receive all that God has made available to you through faith in His Word. Dismiss every thought that does not line up with what God has said. Meditate on the promises and not the problem. Whenever you face situations that threaten to disrupt your confidence or peace, remember to speak the faith-filled Word of God only.

This devotional was designed to provide you with the ammunition needed to stand on the promises of God as your final authority regardless of the circumstances.

I understand that this perspective may be very different from what you've heard or been taught. That's the reason I was led to include so much Word in this book. It's because I know that the evidence found in the rightly divided Word of truth will destroy any doubts you may have about God's love for you.

Faith comes by hearing; however, doubt is a byproduct of hearing anything that doesn't produce faith. So if you're in church but not receiving the rightly divided Word of faith, the things of God will not operate in your life because everything God has promised can only be manifested by faith. Unfortunately, no Word equals no faith.

Ask Holy Spirit to direct you to the truth of the Word of God and receive all that God has made available by His grace through faith in what Jesus has done as our divine substitute. Freely it has been given, freely receive. Be Blessed!

Salvation

If you have never accepted Jesus Christ as your personal Savior, this is an ideal time to do that. You don't have to wait until you get yourself together because the truth is, we can't get ourselves together without God's help. He sent Christ to position us to receive forgiveness for sin and direction into the life He desires for each of us.

God is not angry with you, He wants to be a loving Father to you, and His grace has made that possible through faith in the Blood of Jesus the Christ.

Please repeat after me:

Father God, thank You for sending Jesus to pay for my sins and redeem me from the curse of the law. I accept Him as my personal Savior and Lord of my life. I believe that He died, was buried and resurrected, and is seated with God in heaven as my representative in Jesus' name, Amen.

Thank you for praying that prayer and welcome to the family. Now find a church that teaches the Word of God with clarity and precision and begin to read the Bible for yourself, ask Holy Spirit to guide you. Be Blessed!

About the Authors

Robert and Debra Johnson have been married over thirty years. They are parents of three and grandparents of two. Currently, they are Atlanta residents who have been active in service and ministry for thirty-plus years. Robert holds a degree in Christian Education and is an ordained minister, author, public speaker, and businessman. His focus is to impact the Body of Christ with accurate biblical insight. Debra is an author and committed student of the Bible; her focus is reaching children through stories and pictures with practical biblical lessons. They both agree that Proverbs 4:7, getting understanding of the Word of God, should be the primary objective of every believer.

Acknowledgments

I want to acknowledge some of the people and organizations that have and continue to be sources of growth and spiritual education in my journey.

I cannot say enough about World Changers International Church; my pastors, Creflo and Taffi Dollar, and the anointed team of ministers and teachers at WCCI that pour into believers like us worldwide. Thank you so much for having the courage to obey God in teaching the Gospel according to Grace during a time where religion is increasing in the church and tradition has often taken precedence over the Word of God.

Thank you, Dr. Orr, Robyn Norwood, and the entire staff at WCBS for your uncompromising commitment to preparing those who have accepted the call by equipping us with the tools to do Kingdom business.

To Achieving Excellence Toastmasters Club, thank you for setting me on this journey by helping me to develop my voice and giving me a safe space to grow. I am so grateful that God led me to you, and I thank you for receiving me with a spirit of excellence.

To my TAGG Ministry Partners, Bobby, Danielle, Matt, Sheneen, and Vanessa, thank you for being the iron that sharpens iron, and the steel that sharpens steel. I thank God for you.

Be Blessed!

Prayer Journal

Made in the USA
Columbia, SC
09 February 2021

32713431R00079